W9-BAJ-751

VENUS IN SPURS

SHEILA GILLOOLY

Venus in Spurs

The Secret Female Fear

of Commitment, or

Why You Head for the Hills When Love

Comes to Town

An Owl Book

HENRY HOLT AND COMPANY   NEW YORK

Henry Holt and Company, Inc.
Publishers since 1866
115 West 18th Street
New York, New York 10011

Henry Holt ® is a registered
trademark of Henry Holt and Company, Inc.

Copyright © 1996 by Sheila Gillooly
All rights reserved.
Published in Canada by Fitzhenry & Whiteside Ltd.,
195 Allstate Parkway, Markham, Ontario L3R 4T8.

Library of Congress Cataloging-in-Publication Data
Gillooly, Sheila.
Venus in spurs: the secret female fear of commitment,
or why you head for the hills when love comes to town /
Sheila Gillooly—1st ed.
p.   cm.
1. Man–woman relationships.   2. Commitment
(Psychology).   3. Women—Psychology.   I. Title.
HQ801.G46   1996   95-32623
155.3'33—dc20   CIP

ISBN 0-8050-3552-4
ISBN 0-8050-5355-7 (An Owl Book: pbk.)

Henry Holt books are available for special promotions
and premiums. For details contact: Director, Special Markets.

First published in hardcover in 1996 by
Henry Holt and Company, Inc.

First Owl Book Edition—1997

Designed by Kate Nichols

Printed in the United States of America
All first editions are printed on acid-free paper.∞

            3   5   7   9   10   8   6   4   2
        1   3   5   7   9   10   8   6   4   2   (pbk.)

*For Marie Gillooly,
and for James Spione*

Contents

Acknowledgments   **xi**

PART 1

1: Pleased to Meet Me   **3**

2: The Monster in Me   **14**

3: Why Us, Why Now?   **24**

4: The Second Mrs. de Winter in Spurs:
Female Commitment-Phobes and the Media   **39**

PART 2: Profiles

5: Jesus Wept: The Lure of the Unavailable Man   **69**

6: Ordinary People Moments: Commitment Phobia
and Control   **93**

7: A Pound of Flesh: How Female Commitment-Phobes
Make Bathing Suit Anxiety Work for Us   **118**

8: Portrait of the Artist As a Young Commitment-Phobe: Female Creativity As a Route to Relationship Avoidance   **142**

9: Free Birds: Commitment Anxiety and the Dream of the Remade Self   **161**

PART 3

10: The Fabulous Commitment Quiz   **189**

11: Key to the Fabulous Commitment Quiz   **196**

12: Conclusion   **197**

Acknowledgments

A book such as this one relies as heavily on other people's stories as on my own, so first I'd like to offer my warmest thanks to all the women who bared their souls in order to be profiled for this book. I am fortunate to have such interesting, colorful friends, all of whom allowed me to call them at three in the morning to confirm the details of various romantic travails and who turned the research phase of this book into a lengthy and endlessly enjoyable cocktail party.

I am also fortunate in having been born into one family—and welcomed into another—where human behavior is a source of constant fascination and analysis. Suffice it to say that I learned everything I know about people at my mother's ever-expanding kitchen table, the locus of a continuous roundtable symposium on the vagaries and wonders of human nature. This group includes my mother and late father, Marie and Robert Gilfooly; my grandmother and late grandfather, Mary and William Clancy; Claire, Charlie, Kerry, Caitlin, and Hilary Rose; Dennis, Christine, and Liza Jane Gilfooly; Ellen Gilfooly and Michael Schrier; Elisabeth Gilfooly and R.J.

Connelly; Shirley Edwards; Mary, Mark, and Elizabeth Trivett; Michele, Sheldon, Daniel, and Elijah Stowe; and James Spione.

Many friends have offered love and support during periods of shocking crankiness: Brad Allen, Paul Aviles, Bob Barnett, Tracy Behar, Matt Bertron, Jill Bock, Lewis Brindle, Maureen Brogan, Trudy Brown, Carlo Calzolaio, Paul Croft, Carl Davis, Mara Eilenberg, David Feldman, Karen Fish, Jaqueline Fried, Peter Galvin, Tracey Garet, Lisa Gray, Jeanne Heifetz, Leonardo Iturregui, Robert Jones, Aida Khalil, Richard Kot, JoEllen Kwiatek, Eileen Ledwith, Allen Lyons, Leslie and Evie Lyons, Matt Malloy, Lauren Marino, Christian McLaughlin, James McManus, Susan Mitchell, Mark Mravic, Suzanne Noli, Cathleen O'Connor, Tom O'Connor, Christe Orzechowski, Joyce Pensato, Constantine Photopoulos, Mary Prlain, David Rakoff, Karen Rinaldi, Edward Ruchalski, Lawrence Schrier, Margaret Steele, Pamela Stewart, Scott Treimel, Doug Webster, Trip Weil, Nina Wugmeister, John Young.

When the gods were assigning editors and agents to hapless writers, I was the clear victor. Jennifer Unter is a revelation of sagacity and generosity who wields her red pencil with great intelligence and kindness. Gordon Kato, literary agent extraordinaire, is the sort of genius who manages to marry a discerning aesthetic sensibility with impressive business acumen. He is also in possession of a wildly eclectic and exciting CD collection.

And finally, of course, Richard Whitesell who, though he is not with me, is always with me.

PART 1

1

Pleased to Meet Me

O N THE NIGHT I came into the world, my father hurried down to the hospital nursery to get a gander at his freshly scrubbed and swaddled infant. Wrapped in pink, nestled in my tiny bassinet, I was the very picture of a little lady. My father, who would eventually have four of them, pressed his forehead against the newly Windexed glass and smiled, "Another daughter. Another wedding."

Boy, did he have it wrong.

The fear of commitment may not be a new concept, but never has it been more prevalent, or passionately embraced, than in the last few decades. As this particular affliction has reached epidemic proportions, it has become easy to view commitment anxiety—that sudden, powerful, and mystifying impulse to bolt from a really good thing as if one had been doused with gasoline and set on fire—as an entirely male invention. Men are, after all, the ones who rely openly on this excuse to stave off the threat of romantic responsibility, the horror of intimacy, the peskiness of having to uphold the social contract. They do. You know it.

The woeful truth is that men don't even bother to be embarrassed about their reluctance to get involved in long-term relationships. This disinclination is viewed as a birthright, an exclusively masculine and rather extended rite of passage that ensures men a wild and unencumbered youth. It's a little ritual that also manages to guarantee their female peers an intimate relationship with anxiety and Häagen-Dazs, as well as a standing date most Saturday nights with a down comforter and the Not-Ready-for-Prime-Time Players.

Except it's not that simple. When it comes to the fear of commitment, men get all the press, but as it turns out, women aren't exactly what you'd call immune. So powerful is the female urge to ignore our own conflicted emotions, however, that most women are clueless about the fact that we suffer from the same feelings of ambivalence and uncertainty that we battle so valiantly from the other side. Put another way, women may not have the name, but we surely have the game.

That women can suffer unknowingly from commitment anxiety is astounding when you consider how obsessed we are with the subject. Speak to nearly any woman in her twenties or thirties and she'll admit that some significant portion of her life has been spent engaged in strategic planning sessions aimed at reversing the commitment-phobic actions of the entire male population. The topic of emotionally unavailable men is possibly the strongest common bond among females: I have walked into rooms teeming with absolute strangers and in a matter of thirty seconds experienced profound communion with another woman simply by raising my eyebrow in the direction of a particularly James Deaned male specimen.

Our attention to the topic is like a second full-time job, and unlike our salaried one, it's a job for which we would never consider feigning a cold and calling in sick. The possibility, however minute, of missed opportunity would simply be too painful to consider. Everything in our lives—from the excruciatingly playful couples-strewn Levi's jeans commercials to the ubiquitous greeting ("What, no ring yet?") that kicks off every family gathering—conspires to convince us that romantic involvement is essential to the fabric of our existence.

Throughout history, a woman without a man has been viewed as something of a disaster. Take a glance at the Old Testament, and you'll see references all over the place to widows and orphans. In ancient times, it seems, a woman without a man, like a child without a father, was more or less a sitting duck. Time passed, and plagues and locusts were gradually replaced by the more modern calamities of abject poverty, starvation, and alienation; but regardless of the century, the single girl has never been perceived as being particularly high on the food chain. And so, roughly from the time that Christianity burst on the scene and made mincemeat of the Druids with their female-worshiping tendencies, we Western women have grimly accepted our place in the patriarchy. And in patriarchies, as everyone knows, women want to get married.

Love and marriage, the song tells us. A sweet sentiment, but the cold fact has traditionally been marriage and some modicum of power—economic power, power in the community, power in terms of both religious and political law—all transferred to women through their husbands. No wonder marriage is an undertaking women have traditionally embraced with utter seriousness—curling their hair and nervously dieting down to the perfect bridal fighting weight. Rare were the women radical enough to eschew common wisdom and expectation by choosing to remain single, and I suspect a goodly number of them had trust funds secreted away in some Swiss bank account. The rest of us solemnly upheld our part of the social contract, devoting a significant portion of our fantasy life to the number of bridesmaids we would choose and whether the natural glories of an outdoor ceremony outweighed the risk of inclement weather.

But something unexpected happened a couple of decades ago, and that something was the women's movement. My generation didn't know it, sitting in our high chairs and flinging mashed bananas at the wall, but our older sisters were changing the rules. By the time I went to college in 1980, nearly every woman I knew anticipated finishing her education and going on to some unspeakably glamorous, what-color-is-your-parachute sort of job. I'm not suggesting that our worlds were not ruled by romance and its devastations, but we genuinely believed that we would eventually race off and become journalists or financial analysts or lawyers.

And we did. Nearly every woman I knew eventually landed a job in her area of interest, and we accepted this as our due. We didn't give a lot of thought to the fact that twenty years ago it might not have happened. That maybe the sort of jobs we were seeking and being offered weren't available to women too many years before we burst onto the collegiate scene with its beer balls and inordinate weight gain. Where once we were helpmeets, ornaments, a species who considered the only viable professions to be teaching or nursing ("So, you'll meet a doctor!"), we suddenly became competition. We went out and purchased a single navy suit (skirt modestly cut just above the knee) and lined up with the boys when the corporate recruiters arrived on campus. Clutching our résumés and GPAs we moved to cities and met with personnel officers and smiled politely. We got the jobs.

But it turns out that cultural transformation isn't free. Feminism encouraged female assertiveness and ambition, but because women are still socialized, at least emotionally, to equate success with pleasing others—and specifically with attracting a man—we've just channeled all that ambitious energy into figuring out what the man we desire wants and how we can provide it. The more uncooperative the man, the more brilliantly focused we become on getting him to behave. Which, unfortunately, has suited women just fine, given that we have a horrendously difficult time concentrating on ourselves to begin with. Consider our role models—our mothers, those masters of self-effacement, who may or may not have held down jobs, but who always had dinner on the table at six sharp anyway. Never mind if they were cranky or exhausted or just didn't feel like it, they were trained, and they usually trained us, to think of others first.

The common perception of the commitment issue is that it is

inherently gender-divided. Women want security and involvement, and men don't. You would think we'd know better than to subscribe to such a reductive and divisive theory. The blood and guts of the issue, naturally, is more blurred. One of the critical goals of feminism was to teach women to respect our own ambitions and desires. This was a lesson, however well-intentioned, that split women neatly in two. Intellectually, we appreciated being given permission to focus on our personal development and self-actualization. Emotionally, we should have known that change was not going to be so easy.

In the aftermath of the sexual revolution, women suddenly could sleep with men before marriage without having to face being stoned to death the next morning in the town square. However, once sex became freely available, men who might in the past have been more amenable to the notion of commitment when it was the only clear pathway to the bedroom began to see that there was considerably more flexibility in this area. Commitment became an option, something they could consider and, if they wished, disregard. However progressive women might be in theory, the practical reality of all this free love is extremely uncomfortable. When men sleep with us and then decide they don't want to be involved, we tend to feel rejected. I realize I'm generalizing, but for most women I know, sex simply isn't a lighthearted subject.

The options offered by the sexual revolution proved particularly useful to all the young men who felt discomfited by the game of musical chairs that gender roles had been playing in recent years. These same options were considerably less viable for young women. The sexual revolution was hardly revolutionary for women; it offered a superficial adjustment of the rules without changing any of the fundamental tenets of the game. The culture continued to encourage women to be romance validated, while at the same time dramatically changing the guidelines for achieving that validation. In the past, men had been taught to view a woman's sexual availability to them as something valuable or significant; suddenly such availability was viewed as de rigueur, a given, an event that signified nothing more than an opportunity for healthy physical gratification. Put out, ladies, but don't expect a callback. And as this particular development was couched in the rhetoric of equality, women didn't even have the option of responding to it with indignation. By requesting equality, it appeared that we had invited this turn of events. Little wonder that casual sex leaves women feeling horrible. It's like getting a great buy on an unassembled piece of furniture and discovering that the instructions included with it are written in Japanese.

The shifting of gender roles can be a terribly confusing enterprise, and, indeed, we have gotten confused. We are leading double lives: We're ascending the corporate ladder at Olympian speed, we're leading medical research teams, but when we walk to a newsstand to pick up a copy of *U.S. News & World Report*, we pause first to flip through the latest issue of *Bride's* magazine. Most of the women I met in graduate school admitted that they'd dragged their weary selves out of bed at four A.M. to watch Lady Diana get hitched across the Atlantic. Didn't you?

We've all heard about backlash a great deal lately. Susan Faludi has spent months—years, perhaps—compromising her eyesight reading the tiny print of bibliographies and microfiche printouts to reveal the troubling economic disparity between the sexes that is one aspect of this cultural backlash. Unfortunately, the backlash has had as many personal implications as it has economic. And one of its most significant personal implications is bound up with the very ambition we women have been encouraged to develop. We went out and got jobs, jobs that had previously existed solely within the boys' domain, and—surprise—the boys got irritated. And it was those same boys who evened the score, consciously or not, by putting a new spin on the old game of emotional withholding. Forced to engage us professionally, they retaliated by withdrawing romantically. Commitment was a game they could—and did—refuse to play.

So, this is the environment in which a whole generation of young women have come of age. Commitment anxiety is the angry god, the anathema, the dreaded curse of every woman who rushed home from school each afternoon in order to officiate at Barbie's wedding in her basement. We read *Young Miss*, and then we read *Glamour*, and we saw the jubilant, slender models spending carefree afternoons on the playground swings with their adoring boyfriends. Yes, we were being encouraged to take our academic pursuits seriously, but never for a moment were we allowed to forget that we would be judged by an even higher standard than precocious braininess; we would be judged, and harshly, by our attractiveness to men.

Early on, we imagined that ours was a reasonable expectation: We could be ambitious, and we could be in love. Soon enough, however, we had an inkling that something had gone terribly wrong. The men, those nice young men who were supposed to have been just as anxious as we to roughhouse on the playground and then, when the time came, to look on admiringly as we applied another coat of Bonne Bell lip gloss, simply weren't up to it. Nor were they up to it later on, in college, when we wanted to whip their butts on the biology final and then have them accompany us to the spring formal. But they especially weren't up to it when all the academic niceties were behind us and we were standing side by side at the office coffee machine, or bumping flirtatiously into one another at some nightclub. We wanted boyfriends, and they weren't ready for (drumroll) "anything serious."

Now, I'm no social scientist, I'm just a person who's been known to throw up on the telephone receiver when her latest paramour announces that it's time to move on. But I am able to recognize that growing up amid so much anxiety and perceived deprivation can lead to a fairly warped sense of priorities. Though our academic or professional achievements were satisfying and pleasant, we, following the well-worn path of human nature, became fixated on what we didn't have. No matter how many accolades or prizes were heaped upon us, we'd take our trophies and go home, forlornly wondering why the guy seated next to us hadn't leaned over to ask for our phone number.

So fixated were we on turning the tides—on forcing the men we liked to realize that love and intimacy were good things, wonderful things—that we never bothered to check on our own internal maelstrom. I speak for myself and many others when I say that it honestly did not occur to us that we might also have felt conflicted about the very same issues that the men were busy citing as the reasons they could not get involved in serious relationships, issues such as the fear of being vulnerable or having difficulty with intimacy. As fears go, they're actually not so difficult to understand— when you enter a relationship you're not only laying yourself bare, you're also accepting responsibility for another person's happiness. What does seem fairly obvious, though, is the fact that these fears don't follow any inherent gender division. They spur men and women alike into fits of apoplexy.

If women are in fact unacknowledged masters of ambivalence—giving passionate lip service to their desire for relationships while secretly avoiding, even sabotaging, potential involvements right and left—perhaps their experience mirrors the contradictions inherent to the cultural changes of the past few decades, specifically those pertaining to shifting gender roles. At the same time that we were having it drummed into our heads that what we wanted, as individuals, as women, was absolutely legitimate, around us we could see quite plainly that in many ways our roles as females were not changing at all. Sure, we were encouraged to excel in the classroom, but we were also expected to watch our older sisters with hair-fine attention as they applied mascara in preparation for a big date. In other words, we were still in training, the old-fashioned kind of training, to be girls. Women have learned a great deal about duplicity from our culture; it's not especially surprising that we have become adept at keeping secrets from ourselves, even about something as apparently straightforward as our romantic availability.

As long as we continue to deceive ourselves about our powerful ambivalence concerning romantic involvement, we will reinforce our perception of ourselves as victims. It's a subject that's gotten a lot of press lately, as Camille Paglia and Katie Roiphe vie for the title of queen of the movement against self-perpetuated female subordination. I'll toss another log on the fire and say that I think women's perception of themselves as victims of the male fear of commitment is alarmingly inaccurate. Inaccurate and ultimately destructive, given the amount of attention it encourages women—who are already inclined in this direction to begin with—to place on someone other than ourselves. We've been given permission to excel in areas other than housework, but we cannot truly inhabit our accomplishments or even effectively know or understand ourselves because we've traded the possibility of self-discovery for the more traditional compulsion to secure love. And once we do find that elusive love, we also find that we've neglected essential aspects of our development and our lives by placing so much importance on the rehabilitation of an uncooperative man.

Having been crucified innumerable times on the wooden cross of love gone wrong, I'm hardly one to glorify the commitment-phobic man. The decade of my twenties was like a slow-motion stroll through the ninth level of Dante's Inferno, and there's virtually not a reward you could offer that would tempt me to return to that time. That said, however, it does seem possible to me that while women are holding impromptu congresses all over the country on conquering male romantic phobias, men are very likely immersed—at least part of the time—in the more substantive struggle of trying to know and understand themselves. I've heard many times, and often said it myself, that young men are self-involved. But if self-involvement can even occasionally result in self-knowledge, can it really be a wholly bad thing?

One of the little-discussed aspects of commitment anxiety is its inherent wisdom as a position. Why do we imagine we can effectively choose a mate before we've had a chance to get to know ourselves? And beyond that, why do we imagine that romantic involvement is going to be an experience of unadulterated rapture? Intimacy isn't easy. It requires us to be vulnerable, to feel pain, to challenge our well-worn and blissfully safe assumptions about ourselves; it requires us to make compromises and sacrifices that simply are not necessary when we are having an imaginary relationship with a glossy photo in a movie magazine or a guy in the apartment down the hall who would be hard-pressed to remember our first name. On a certain level, we're right to be afraid, or at least wary and circumspect.

Around the time that I turned thirty, a very peculiar thing started to happen. One by one, all the women who had accompanied me through the dark days of the previous decade, including myself, met men. We met men, generally very nice men, who wanted to get involved with us. They took us out for dinner and draped their leather jackets over our shoulders when the evening turned chilly. They stayed over for two nights in a row. We waited anxiously for the other shoe to drop, but, lo, it did not. The men we were meeting were sincere in their desire to engage in serious adult relationships.

So, does it surprise you to learn that, after all the fanfare and celebration had subsided, it was the women in these couples who began to evidence difficulty making a commitment? Our partners, after all, had spent the previous ten or fifteen years attending to concerns other than romantic turmoil. They had struggled equally with career choices, family issues, compelling questions of identity. They were now ready to confront their well-examined fears of intimacy and trust. And we women? Only when we had attained romantic security could we relax enough to begin to make the critical distinction between fantasy and reality and choose between the two. And what's more, we were forced to face all the other aspects of our lives and selves that we had allowed to languish for so many years. It turned out that we had a hell of a lot of catching up to do.

For me, it was necessary to become involved in a serious relationship before I could begin to acknowledge the minefield of fears underlying my fierce determination to do so. It wasn't until I'd tasted coveted security that I could relax enough to view my compulsive behavior with any clarity or insight. But that needn't be the case. It's perfectly fine and reasonable to want a boyfriend. However, when the quest for a relationship supersedes every other goal, what we've got is a fairly clear indication that our anxieties about the other, more urgent questions in life are being displaced onto the romance issue. And while this denial is allowed to snowball unchecked, not only do we remain estranged from our actual selves, but we also seriously impede the progress in those other critical areas of self-development that profoundly affect not only our eventual relationships, but every aspect of our lives.

2

The Monster in Me

I REMEMBER WITH PECULIAR VIVIDNESS the first man who ever captured my heart. Peculiar, because I was about eighteen months old when the love bug bit me. There I was, diapered, beach ball in hand, sneaking across the boundary between my yard and his, anxious to get some playdate action going. Family lore has it that my beleaguered young father actually took the day off from work to build a fence strong enough to keep me safely caged up. Such was my determination to commune with my true love, however, that by the time my father completed the fence's construction, I had successfully learned to scamper over it.

That was the beginning. The beginning of the end, really. My first heartthrob, a four-year-old Don Giovanni (or Brian O'Connor, as we knew him), was about to teach me a lasting lesson in the horrors of the platonic ideal. He didn't have the language down—that would come later—but one doesn't necessarily have to be fluent or, it turns out, even verbal to recognize the "let's be friends" speech when one hears it. It was clear that my beloved, fond though he was of me, felt it best that we enjoy each other's company with no particular strings attached. Needless to say, I felt otherwise. But I didn't give up. Oh, no, quite the contrary: I had fallen off the horse and, like any good sport, I was willing to hop back on.

When I was five, my family moved. Rather than experiencing grief at leaving my infant home, I was elated at the prospect of a brand new neighborhood virtually teeming with potential romantic possibilities. Before my mother could tell the movers where to set the well-packed boxes of china, I had already discovered that the family next door had three sons. Three! I climbed onto the banana seat of my new bike and rode up and down the street like a triumphant goddess, happily imagining all the many new acquaintances I was about to make.

Well, I did make those acquaintances, but they were not the earth-shattering ones I envisioned. The sad truth was that the boys on my street evinced far more passion for Wiffleball and street hockey than they did for romantic liaisons behind our parents' well-tended gardens. The girls they liked were beautiful and remote, and utterly disdainful of any awkward attention the boys might have offered them—a situation that left everyone involved pleasantly unchallenged. It goes without saying that I was not one of those girls. Which is not to say that in my youthful struggles I didn't have a great deal of company. My loyal gang of girlfriends were just as committed as I to penetrating the mysterious world of boys. Little did we know the wonders in store for us.

Time lurched on, and I found myself in the land of formal education, involved in the usual ascension from elementary to junior high to high school. I held firm to my belief that as I aged, the males around me would catch up, that the problem lay in staggered levels of maturity. I was buying the old line that boys grow up less quickly than girls. Time would take care of my romantic conundrum, I believed. I was wrong.

Eventually it became clear that the problem had something to do with the kind of guys I liked. I prided myself on not falling strictly for looks; what the men I pursued had in common was their inclination toward brooding. I fell for introspection, a certain dark spirit, a kind of misanthropic creativity—high school's version of the artist, you might say. These guys, with their excessive solitary drinking and their offhand quoting of Kafka, were not exactly easy prey. They had about as much to offer emotionally as a pile of cinderblocks. I sat in my bedroom and set my Joni Mitchell albums on replay and anguished over how to get my love life on the right track.

College, with all its promise of romantic interludes amid vine-strewn gothic buildings, proved a bust. Like many eighteen-year-olds, I was unwise in my selection of schools and found myself matriculated at one whose pickings in the interesting-men department were slim indeed. My fierce, against-all-odds determination to transcend this tragic reality left me, naturally enough, falling in love with homosexuals. My passion for one of these men was so strong that I moved, upon graduation, to his childhood home, plagued with the hope that after he'd finished sowing his wild oats, he'd find his way back there. Does the word *pathetic* seem appropriate here? In any event, once all the consternation and nervous confessions were out of the way, I found myself with several very close friends, but still no great love.

By the time I reached my twenties, I was what you might generously describe as out of control. There was a man out there for me and, goddammit, I was going to find him. I wasn't much different from all the other women I knew. I was possessed, and if you think I don't mean in the style of Linda Blair, you're wrong. Oh, how I wanted a boyfriend. Oh, the agony of not having one. I suffered—sometimes stoically, frequently not—through the mine-field of ordinary social intercourse. Through the hell of weekdays— each jaunt into the office fraught with the possibility that some coworker might announce that she'd been asked on a date, or that a friend might call to say that she (according to her very precise requirements) had lighted upon the perfect man. And each week concluded with a weekend, in particular the dreaded Sunday morning: climbing out of my empty, chilly bed, throwing on my mother's discarded winter coat, and, with great determination, descending the stairs in search of a newspaper and a miserly cup of coffee. Did I have amnesia? Had I simply forgotten the previous Sunday, barely seven days ago, when I'd made this same journey? Because, as any single woman knows, Sunday morning is postdate morning, and all the extravagantly lucky girls who managed to get some guy to commit to a Saturday night and stay over would be bundling up and traipsing out for a leisurely hungover breakfast à deux in some darling coffee shop around the corner. The mere sight of these glowing twosomes was enough to push even the most stalwart of us over the edge.

I'm not suggesting that I sat at home every night. Far from it, sorry to say, for I was nothing if not committed to my mission. I continued to believe—in spite of a calamitously long list of relationships I'd managed to get going only to watch, stunned, as they ran themselves smack into bridge abutments—that the right man, the man who would conquer his fears about the deadly requirements of intimacy, was out there. Do I need to tell you that I wasn't always picky? That I practiced the art of keeping an open mind the way a Zen master would his koan? Sure, I loved it when a suitor who could string two sentences together came knocking on my door, but the truth is, it wasn't a requirement. Hey, maybe my current beau had just gotten out of prison, but it seemed perfectly possible that his had been a white-collar crime. He was ambitious, and who can blame a man for that? I dated wonderful men and I dated pond scum, and all of them, by some alarming convergence of physics gone very wrong, shared one characteristic: They couldn't make a commitment.

And then the unimaginable happened: I met The One. Just the week before, I had had my heart severed in two hideous halves by a man who had appeared to be so mature and thoughtful that I literally couldn't understand the words when he announced that he was feeling a little crowded and thought he needed some space. Oh, and he had slept with a mutual friend of ours. Had he mentioned that? So, I was reeling from this news, just that little bit closer to taking a book on bomb-making out of the library and cooking up a little surprise for his car ride home, when I up and met The One.

Now, you'll laugh, but I must continue. As luck would have it, an early flirtatious conversation had revealed that The One was not only previously engaged, but he was living with his previous engagement and had been for several years. Was it significant that he was unavailable? Of course it was. Because, otherwise involved as he was, I did not consider him romantic fodder. Yes, I toyed momentarily with the movie-of-the-week drama of stealing another's man, but it wasn't really an option that appealed to me. Ultimately, what this arrangement really managed to do was to trick me into seeing this man as a person rather than a potential conquest.

Don't be disappointed: It got ugly. Once I began to see him as a person, all the objectified fantasies I'd been happily having were replaced by the real thing. And in case you haven't been down this particular path yet, the real thing can be mighty unpleasant. All the beautiful control you've convinced yourself that you have, that indeed you do have while engaged in relationships with phantoms, evaporates. And difficult as our increasing and illicit devotion was for all the obvious reasons, true catastrophe arrived in the form of my new beau's announcement that this infatuation thing was all well and good, but he thought the time had come for him to hightail it home and work on the relationship he was actually having. So, I found The One and then promptly lost him.

Imagine my surprise when—not six months later—the gods smiled on me. The telephone rang and I picked it up to find The One on the other end, explaining that his relationship had come to the conclusion he had suspected it would and was I free to have dinner with him that night? As it turned out, I was.

For me, the reality of finally being in a relationship was a revelation. I took nothing for granted: Every time my beloved appeared on my doorstep, trumpets sounded and champagne corks blew off every bottle in a five-mile radius. I had a boyfriend! I had a normal boyfriend! Someone capable of, say, reading a newspaper and discussing its contents. I remember the pure relief flooding my oldest sister's face the first time she met my intended. Finally, her expression said, someone who isn't going to try to steal the silver.

So I was happy, and I was also wary. I assumed my new role of girlfriend, I made sure I had coffee in the house for those lazy Sunday mornings in and out of bed, but I hadn't forgotten the lessons of my recent past. To my surprise, though, nothing terrible happened. No horrible revelations, no letters from the parole board tumbling out of his briefcase, no bumping into him out on a date with someone else. In time, we decided to move in together, and you can imagine the astonishment with which I greeted that little development. I made room in my shoebox of an apartment, happily tossing out furniture and clothing that I had once deemed essential to my ability to draw breath. In he moved, and together we began the mutual journey of domestic bliss.

Too good to be true? You bet. But this time, the monster did not arrive in masculine form. That would have been too easy. No, what happened was that all the tiny seeds of sedition that had been lying dormant in me for approximately thirty years suddenly sprouted. There we sat, cozily passing evenings reading by soft lamplight, he sipping a glass of wine and I choking on bitter thoughts about all the many things that I was missing out on. How was it that as we sat down to yet another perfectly planned and prepared dinner, my thoughts would turn longingly to the nights I'd stood in front of my open refrigerator spooning mouthfuls of cottage cheese and chives? Irony of ironies, it appeared that the man of my dreams was far more comfortable with the day-to-day emotional requirements of togetherness than I was.

Which left me baffled. The tiny angelic voice of perseverance that had trilled away continuously in my brain for all these years had been replaced by a low rumble of rebellion and resentment. I had gotten what I wanted; what was I complaining about? Picking up the telephone at the office to hear the dulcet voice of my beloved asking what I'd like to do that evening, I'd feel my throat close under the pressure of some phantom grip and hiss, "I have plans!" before slamming the receiver down. The shift in me from grateful recipient of love to disagreeable, demanding she-devil was swift and mysterious and made my situation at home a little, shall we say, tense. It wasn't that my feelings for my partner had diminished. As time passed, in fact, they had grown deeper and stronger. In rare moments of sanity, I'd glance across the room and see him bathed in the warm light of the fireplace and think, "What's wrong with me? He's wonderful." No, it seemed that my problem had to do with something else. I was discovering in myself a powerful fear, a fear of none other than my old pal commitment.

I was learning a lesson that I had managed to avoid for all my many years in training—that being emotionally responsible to another person is a demanding task. It requires a far deeper investment than the highly dramatic fantastical entanglements of my single days. I had been so anxious to get rid of my autonomy and privacy that I'd never for a second considered their value. I had never considered that my ridiculous romantic choices might have been undertaken (at least in part) in an ingenious effort to safeguard these aspects of my existence. I began to come to the troubling conclusion that all those dead-end, high-maintenance, non-relationships might have had more in common than sheer bad luck. And however uncomfortable this realization was, it was so true that I couldn't deny it: By frantically entertaining this string of go-nowhere liaisons, I had been avoiding the commitment issue as effectively as had all the men who lost my phone number after the third date.

In finding a mate, I'd found someone to share my days and nights, and the rewards inherent in this were many and glorious. I'd also lost my focus, which was more than a little unnerving. Sustaining a healthy relationship, however demanding, simply didn't require the same intensity, the same brilliant resourcefulness, that taming an untamable man had. No more nights conversing for hours on the telephone with friends, trying to determine the true meaning of that greeting I had shared with a man in the laundry room of my building. I was now expected to have actual conversations with my beau—we were required to relate. He opened his mouth and told me exactly what he was thinking. Where was the intrigue? The delicious, agonizing mystery? Without the passionate anguish of my mission, I found that I was no longer sure who I was.

And something else, something even stranger, began to happen. Lots of other elements of my life that had felt perfectly comfortable before the change in my living situation suddenly started to chafe. I'd open my eyes each morning—just about the time I was supposed to arrive at the office—and wonder why I was dragging myself out of a warm bed to travel to a job I could tolerate only because of the daily promise of spending fifteen minutes sitting in my boss's office smoking cigarettes and debating the best recipe for lemon pound cake. I began to examine other aspects of my existence: friendships that I'd allowed to languish or grow stale because I'd been, frankly, much too busy to attend to them; difficult issues in my family that I had blithely avoided trying to resolve; even some of the pain of coming to terms with my father's death. All the things that had been put on the back burner while the manhunt was under way reared their ugly heads, all at once it seemed.

When my central goal in life was finding a man, my life shaped itself around this quest. I became and remained focused on my goal, and everything else fell away. Because this goal involved controlling or changing another person's behavior—in my case, any number of commitment-phobic men—I was virtually able to ignore my own actions, at least those that didn't pertain directly to the response of the other person. This was an incredibly safe position to be in. All the usual and difficult work of life—getting to know myself, pursuing genuinely satisfying work, engaging in rewarding non-romantic involvements—was cast to the side so that the real goal, the goal of romantic fulfillment, could be attained.

When I finally attained that goal, I found myself sitting in a field of rubble. Romantic love, incredible as it was, did not supply enough material for a full life. I was devastated to see all that I had left to fester untended and ignored for such a long time. Having finally gotten what I'd so badly wanted, I began to recognize the extent to which my furious efforts to find true love had been a way of distracting myself from the critical—and hugely intimidating— questions of who I wanted to be and how I planned to get there.

In my case, attention to the issue of commitment anxiety kept me from another issue I obviously didn't wish to face and am still in the process of facing now. It has to do with a commitment to one's self. When I pinned all my expectations on another person, I was letting myself completely off the hook. The importance and consequences of my own choices and behavior, my successes and failures, were eclipsed by my attention to the actions of other people, specifically those of the men I was pursuing. It was painful to put aside the camouflage and try to get to know myself and understand what I wanted. It required, for one thing, leaving a job that made me feel secure in order to make a serious effort to write—something I'd always imagined I'd do but never found the time for, what with all the lying on the couch and crying I had to accomplish first. But the satisfactions along this route feel much more substantial to me than the "victories"—such as getting a guy to call when he says he will—of the past.

And speaking of the victories of the past, what impact do these revelations have on the relationships we've undertaken? If you wait until you're actually in a relationship to discover your own ambivalence about being there, there's no question that this discovery will change things. No matter what slavish and subordinate behavior we may be culturally brainwashed into undertaking on the path toward romantic involvement, the point of being in a real relationship is to be a member of a two-person team. Otherwise what you're calling a relationship is in fact unpaid employment. If the man you've become involved with can't handle your new struggle for selfhood, he's looking for a personal assistant, not a lover.

Which is not to say it will always be easy. My boyfriend experienced moments of sheer horror as my new, thorny self began to emerge. There were things about that woman, who was constantly baking popovers and shaving her legs, that genuinely pleased him and times, I know, when he regretted her passing. He'd consented to move in with a bona fide Stepford Wife, and found instead that he was living with the chest-burster from *Alien*—complete with all the writhing and screeching. My good-girl reserves had gotten very low, it seemed, and there was a whole not-so-nice spectrum in me waiting to be explored. Which might tell you something about what I'd been unwilling to face during all those years of assiduously avoiding intimacy.

But the difference this time was that if my beau had tried to resist these changes, if he had not ultimately celebrated them right along with me, I know I would have come to a point when his lack of support would have forced me to move on. When I put aside the elaborate distractions of finding someone to love, what I saw was that I already did have someone: myself. I just had to devote myself to figuring out how to accept her, as they say, warts and all. The fear of being alone, and all the troubles this fear creates, diminishes considerably once you begin to recognize the importance of focusing your energy and attention on yourself.

3

Why Us, Why Now?

ABOUT TEN YEARS AGO, during a Christmas break from college, my mother and I had a conversation that I still remember vividly. She had come upon me rifling through my younger sister's closet in search of clothing to steal. Adopting that expression of extreme neutrality parents wear when they discover their children in the midst of petty theft, my mother sat down on my sister's floral comforter and proceeded to act as audience to my informal fashion show. Because my sister has considerably better taste than I do, my mother and I both enjoyed the transformation that occurred as I traded my pilled gray sweat suit for the stylish and costly black crepe jackets suddenly at my disposal. I was banking on that transformation, and not because I'd suddenly become fastidious about my appearance. There was nothing random about this wished-for metamorphosis: I was trying to snag an ambivalent man. Love trouble was mine, and I had come to the sorry point where I was willing to believe what every magazine had been telling me for years: The way to a man's heart is through an improved wardrobe. Certainly nothing else was working.

As I pivoted anxiously before the mirror, I began to share my sad tale with my mother. I was in love, and the object of my affections was demonstrating no particular interest in me. My mother listened as I poured out the pitiful saga of the complicated, greatly nuanced, and ultimately futile minuet this man and I had been engaged in for the past few months. It was clear, even to me, that the relationship was heading nowhere, though this break from school had given me an excellent opportunity to stoke my fantasy's fire.

My mother sat back on the bed, thinking perhaps of the amount of money she was shoveling into the black hole of college tuition while her daughter was firmly entrenched on an extracurricular—and obviously failing—quest for a boyfriend, and said suddenly, "I don't know what it is with all these boys you know. When I was in college, everyone just assumed they were going to get married. The girls and the boys. There was no fear of commitment. Men expected to get married, and they just set about finding the best girl they could to do so with."

My mother's voice was filled with puzzlement. She could see plainly that I was not unusual in my parade of romantic mishaps. The fact that my older sister had married young, at twenty-four, was the exception that proved the rule, for my mother had the example of not just me, but my two younger sisters and our large collective network of friends, from which to conclude that something had changed dramatically in the dynamic between young men and women.

So what happened? That the world is a different place now than when my parents were emerging into adulthood seems almost inarguable. During the second half of this century, we've witnessed some profound changes. There was a time—as recent as my parents' childhood—when life was slightly more predictable, when babies were born into the bosom of large extended families, raised among relatives and lifelong friends, and ended up employed by family businesses or, at the very least, holding jobs that kept them in the same geographical area in which they'd been raised. During this rather extended period of Norman Rockwellian familial bliss, the biggest calamities one could anticipate were the purchase of an automotive lemon or the hostile invasion of one's backyard garden by hungry, self-serving rabbits. Or, on a larger scale, one could lose sleep contemplating the unpleasant possibility of democracy's replacement by some darker form of governmental rule, such as communism, and the fact that such rule, should it arrive, would likely do so in the shape of a disagreeable foreign army plunking itself down on our nation's heretofore apparently inviolate doorstep.

Relatively speaking, though, these were largely abstract worries, until the bombing of Pearl Harbor and the subsequent utilization of the atomic bomb made them very concrete. Suddenly the impossible—the bombing of U.S. territory—became reality. And, with the decimation of select Japanese cities, the A-bomb stepped out of the realm of hypothetical weaponry and, given the nature of reciprocity, made real the possibility of true, planet-exploding global warfare. Our introduction to nuclear contention was just the beginning of the domino game of horrors that has distinguished the second half of our century. We've seen governments topple into bellicose chaos, discovered that aerosol deodorant makes short work of the ozone layer, and endured a refresher course in the term *plague* as throngs of loved ones started dying of one. We've entered the Age of Anxiety, a harrowing and churlish little epoch of which Edith Wharton would most certainly disapprove.

And when you consider that, in addition to these global problems, we are burdened with ever-increasing personal challenges as well—the fact that at an age when we are is barely old enough to vote, we are spirited off to faraway colleges, plunked down many states or even countries away from home, encouraged to accept demanding jobs teeming with unspeakable responsibilities and to live comparatively alienated and transient lives in loud urban centers—it's little wonder that we develop ulcers early and rack up tons of debt on our high-interest credit cards. And yet in spite of these constant dark clouds on the horizon, we are expected to—and indeed do—cope every day with the myriad anxieties and uncertainties these challenges create. The world has changed, expectations have changed, and yet we adapt, we persevere.

Except when it comes to commitment. Men and women alike, however dissimilarly this anxiety is manifested, have grown terrified of selecting a partner and pledging long-term devotion.

The operative phrase in the previous statement is *however dissimilarly this anxiety is manifested*, for it cannot be stressed enough that men and women experience and express this fear differently. As I mentioned earlier, most women are genuinely unaware or extremely reluctant to acknowledge that they fear commitment at all. Those few who have been forced to admit that they suffer thusly treat their problem as though it were an unpleasant medical condition—"I've got to do something about this inability to sustain a relationship"—a malady that only a visit to their physician and a potent-smelling prescription might correct. Conversely, men's admission of their disinclination to commit romantically is accompanied by a certain swagger: "Got rid of another one," they say, and clap their palms briskly together in the universal gesture of a job well done. It's curious to consider that admitting to a fear of romantic involvement does not, like admitting to other fears, threaten masculinity, but rather seems to bolster it, like an appreciation of bikini-clad prancing models on a beer commercial or a particularly blinding victory on the racquetball court.

Although in other areas of our lives we're expected to be bold, industrious, and overflowing with courage, somehow in the romantic arena it is possible to admit to a modicum of timidity. I suspect this has something to do with our culture's enduring love affair with the concept of personal transformation, coupled with the mistaken notion that committing to a romantic partnership has the power to stop this process dead in its tracks. The problem is that, though we are taught to respect and desire this ability to remake ourselves, we often don't know the first thing about achieving it. It seems clear to me now that the romantic square dance many of us perpetuate long after it has become a tired ritual keeps us in a static and unsatisfactory point in our development. To be involved in an intimate relationship actually frees the imagination to discover one's own private potential and affords one the time and energy to do something about getting to that desired place. But I'm getting ahead of myself.

Long ago, before our country became a map of connect-the-dot Gap stores but after the European settlers made the interesting assumption that whatever they laid their eyes on was theirs to keep, our defining national spirit was one of potential transformation. The business about taxation without representation and the cessation of religious persecution was all well and good, but the true draw to all this wild countryside was the romance of the remade life. Open any American history book and behold: People traveled a long distance, docked their boats, and proceeded to alter what was before them — and themselves along with it — into a more acceptable version of life.

The names these settlers chose for their adopted homes say it all: New York, New Bedford, New Haven. The manifesto that later lent itself to an advertising campaign for hair-care products — the same, but better. It's a simple enough notion: Travel to a place where nobody knows you and find yourself released from all previous sins and mistakes. The problem, as these early settlers discovered, was that a brand-new country is eventually a brand-new settled country, and so it was that the westward progression began. As soon as all the really stellar plots along the Eastern Seaboard were grabbed up, settlers started feeling crowded and taking off for parts west. From Boston to San Francisco, the fossilized wagon tracks tell the story of the call of the fresh start.

The desire for a better life is a powerful one, but the desire for a better self is even stronger. And the truth is, we haven't strayed so far from those early settlers, nor has this particular national anthem changed much—Americans believe fervently in personal transformation. These days, unfortunately, it's a little tougher to light upon a suitable transformative challenge, assuming one is unwilling to participate in a triathlon or reserve a bed in Biosphere. All the good land has been settled, and the sort of rugged frontier challenges that once renewed one's faith in oneself and one's capabilities have been reduced to getting a great deal on a rent-controlled apartment or successfully figuring out how to microwave a large potato in less than eight minutes.

This is where our interpersonal relationships step in. Every time we enter a new one we avail ourselves of the possibility of rebirth. All our little quirks and flaws fade away, our limitations and failings disappear, we become whomever we wish to become. Of course this period of personal renewal is not only brief but also fallacious, and sooner or later that pesky person we know as ourself rears his or her remarkably ugly head and starts demanding that things return to their normal and banal way. For months we'll listen to whatever discordant alternative jazz CD our new lover sets on repeat, or we'll pleasantly accompany him or her to experimental foreign-language movies in which there are no subtitles and no need for them because the actors communicate solely through portentous glances. And then one morning we wake up and we're ourselves again, the self that drinks diet Coke for breakfast or religiously watches reruns of *Murder She Wrote* every Thursday night. Gradually our true—and truly pedestrian—self is revealed, and our partner either accepts or rejects it, but ultimately that is not the point. What *is* the point is that regardless of our lover's reaction to the real us, the fact that they've been witness to our true self means that there's no escape. Our lovers, once the catalyst for our splendid metamorphosis, become instead prison wardens whose mere presence is a constant reminder of our captivity. Therefore, we are compelled to begin the process again, weaseling out of our current relationships and into new ones, where we once again experience the possibility of becoming all things. The pioneers had covered wagons and belligerent Indians; we have singles bars and personal ads. But the goal is the same—instant change.

This quick-fix transformation, the sort we imagine will result from a shift in geography, a new job, or a different lover, is necessarily temporary. This is because it's external. Eventually the wilderness is tamed or the mate becomes familiar, and we find ourselves stuck, once again, with ourselves. I remember reading, as a child, some dreary young-adult novel about a pioneer family whose father spent the whole of the story uprooting his wife and children and leading them into more and more difficult and uncomfortable surroundings—first Ohio, then Nebraska, and finally California—each setting more remote and ghastly than the last. The intention of this story was to emphasize the die-hard pioneer spirit, the particularly American hunger for greater and greater challenge. It was designed to impress upon youthful readers the glory of perseverance and the ways in which character is shaped and strengthened. But, reading it, all I could think was, What about the poor wife? That the father was bent not on personal challenge or the triumph of man over nature, but on escape, pure and simple. And meanwhile, the wife was forced every year to pack up her children and her crudely fashioned cooking implements and follow her spouse into ever-more-impossible hardship. It was a tale that said more about compulsion and avoidance than strength of character.

The really prime settling is over. *Northern Exposure*, with its intimation that the inhabitants of the forty-ninth state sit around all day sipping cappuccino and quoting Heidegger, has domesticated Alaska, the last North American frontier. For a while it looked as though the space program might offer an interesting alternative, what with the extraordinary amount of money poured into it and those curiously phallic rockets and its general suggestion that the moon might not be such a bad place to spend the weekend after all. But then *Challenger* exploded, the Hubble telescope almost worked, and, frankly, one realized that diminutive freeze-dried astronaut food was probably not as tasty as a Swanson's Hungry Man fried chicken dinner, available right here on Earth. So—*poof*—the truly final frontier finally seemed like a fairly unattainable one. Home is where we've had to turn for the contemporary version of this ritual enactment of the reborn self, entering and exiting relationships at the speed of light, or at least as soon as some shred of intimacy and demystification is achieved. The only difference now is that men are not alone in their longing for the renewed self. Consciously or not, women are playing right along. If the male of the relationship doesn't make leave-taking noises soon enough, the female will root out some unacceptable aspect of her partner's character that makes defection the only reasonable option.

Later on we will look extensively at the ways in which women rather cleverly indulge this impulse toward flight by avoiding or aborting potential relationships. Men are generally far less covert than their female counterparts in the ways in which they escape the imagined limits imposed by communion with a mate. This is not to say that all men follow the same blueprint of intimacy avoidance. Their methods, as my experience has borne out again and again, can be radically different. Many men prefer to keep their liaisons brief, however intense and promising they might be. Others like to sustain connection long enough that it appears a significant commitment is going to be made, and then jump ship at the critical moment. Allow me to elaborate.

When I was in my mid-twenties, I met a man whom we'll call Michael. Michael was moderately attractive—a pleasant enough face, though not one you'd see splashed across the covers of romance novels. He was what my sisters and I as children would have referred to as a "businessman"—conservative suits, oxblood briefcase, marine-short hair. Michael was tremendously ambitious, employed by one of those mysterious finance companies that became so popular in the eighties, when everyone needed tons of income to purchase condominiums and Danish-made stereo systems. Though young, he had already risen to a sort of midpoint on the corporate ladder, and he clearly believed himself destined for the sort of greatness one in his position might hope to achieve. In other words, he wished—and expected—to get rich.

Michael was very disciplined about his priorities: work first, work second, workout third, excessive beer drinking with male friends fourth, women fifth. A low fifth. For the four or five months we dated, we regarded ours a fairly serious involvement—he because he had to call me more than once a week, and I because I was delusional. It wasn't a big secret that our expectations of a romantic relationship were dramatically different: I devoted countless hours to the internal debate over whether I should keep my name or hyphenate when we married, and he considered himself princely if he showed up for a date on the appointed evening. Michael was someone who was capable of being committed to only one thing at a time, and it became clear rather rapidly that this one thing was his job. His self-worth rested entirely on his performance at the office, and as soon as it became apparent that my expectations represented a potential distraction from his single-minded devotion to his job, he was out the door.

Needless to say, I was devastated. Certainly all the signs had been there; I knew Michael was emotionally unavailable. But somewhere along the line I managed to convince myself that I also held the key to changing his personality: Once he saw how wonderful true love could be, I thought, he would loosen the rigid hold his ambitions had on his jugular. When this turned out not to be the case, I did what any red-blooded American girl would do: lived on chocolate and red wine for two weeks and called every woman I knew so she could tell me how wronged I'd been and how easy a mistake such as mine was to make. I threw myself wholeheartedly into suffering. And when the two weeks were up, I drew a ragged breath, reapplied my mascara, and resumed my search. I believed I had learned a hard lesson with Michael—no more uptight, overly focused career Nazis; this time I would find a man with feelings, a man who not only cared about his interior life but also would want to share it with me. Then I met Brian, and I thought I'd struck gold.

Brian was the polar opposite of Michael—a charming and penniless painter who made his living stretching and hefting the canvases and materials of other more financially solvent associates. Sort of an artist's caddy. He refused to be seen in anything other than jeans and a T-shirt and had long curly hair and a perpetual five o'clock shadow that caused him to resemble either Alec Baldwin or Fred Flintstone, depending on the viewer. He was charmingly unkempt, had the posture of a boiled shrimp, and thought the stock market was a place to which one traveled in order to purchase the ingredients for soup. I was in heaven.

Brian was that rarest of men—he was interested in feelings. My feelings, his feelings, the cat's feelings—the emotional landscape was a source of endless fascination for him. He had been involved in all types of therapy, from couples to scream, and he had the language of psychological exploration down to a science. I luxuriated in the intimate quality of his attention; I felt as though he were responding to something unique and special in me. We'd be standing in the grocery check-out line, with me relating the humiliating details of being dressed down at work for transposing the numbers on a telephone message, and he'd level his sensitive gaze at me and ask, "Were you breastfed?" He wanted, it seemed, to know everything about me—childhood traumas, previous heartbreaks, political biases, everything.

Now, as it happened, Brian lived in another city, some three hours away from the one I lived in. Because the time we did spend together was so nearly perfect—tender and sensuous, passed lazing about our respective apartments talking and drinking wine and eating foods high in fat content—it seemed utterly natural that this distance would start to chafe. If things were so good in spite of the train rides and long-distance phone bills, imagine the bliss we would experience living in the same city—or better, the same apartment. That we were meant to be together was obvious, for he was the man of my dreams, and so in this sweet and innocent way did the dreaded relocation discussions begin.

At first, Brian and I saw eye to eye. Of course one of us should move; of course it was ridiculous to remain apart. He had always wanted to live in New York—it was where the really serious art was happening. New York was one of the few places where people were genuinely alive. He would move. Except there were problems: Money, for one, of which he had none. The professional contacts he'd already made in Baltimore, for another; contacts that—he was quick to remind me—he would simply be giving up were he to move. And finally New York itself, which began to seem to Brian a very threatening city after all.

Well, friends, New York was indeed a threatening city, but not because of its complicated subway system or higher crime rate. New York was threatening because it was the city in which I lived. Brian, as it happened, was deeply fearful of making a commitment to me, to anyone in fact, and eventually I understood that the secret to our success as a couple, the very basis for all of that wonderful, exquisite happiness, was the three hours that lay neatly between us. With that distance squarely in place, Brian could be loving, he could be generous, he could fill my starving little head with promises—promises he probably did wish to keep. But once I requested that we bring our ecstasy into the realm of reality, our relationship became impossible.

The truth is that, as with Michael, there had been signs. Brian was thirty-six, more than ten years older than I, and though he'd had lots of relationships (I should say, lots of women had fallen in love with him), he'd never successfully made a romantic commitment. To be sure, he was considerably more covert about his disinclination toward intimacy—feeding me grapes and euphorically listing all the indisputable reasons that I was the one for him. However, I might have done myself a favor and let history speak for itself.

At the time that I met him, Brian had been seriously painting for almost fifteen years. Objectively, this means very little. Many artists struggle for twice that long or longer before getting the recognition they deserve. However, though he may have known this, such a rationalization meant little to Brian. He was terrified of failure, and he felt that with the years passing, such failure was more and more ensured. I was almost ten years younger than he when we met, at the start of my adult life, in the first job of my career. Whatever complaints I might have had about the lowliness of my position, such entry-level hardships were extremely attractive to him. When we were together, he could forget that he was not also at the beginning of his professional life; he could mentally enter my struggles and make them his own. This must have felt like pure relief, to abandon his own experience, even momentarily, and enter someone else's less-tested travails. It was a satisfying fantasy, but one of its necessary components was a restriction in the amount of time we could actually spend together. I imagine that Brian understood instinctively that once these restraints of distance were removed, he would be face to face with the dissolution of his fantasy, he would once again have to own up to the realities of his difficult and unsatisfying life.

Brian was not afraid of what our involvement would prevent him from becoming; he was afraid of what he already was—a penniless and unrecognized painter who would have given anything to recapture the naive optimism that I, at twenty-five, embodied so firmly.

My relationship with Brian ended rather abruptly when he called me one night to say that he'd slept with a woman whose name I recognized, a woman I'd never met but of whom he'd spoken to me several times. She was younger than I and in the midst of one of those early-twenties periods of hardship—estrangement from her family, cruel abandonment by a lover, imminent eviction. She was a person caught in a maze of what felt to her like tragedy on a grand scale, someone whose operatic troubles would make a much better distraction than my rather pale existentialist confusion. And, even better, at age twenty she hadn't even set foot in the world of adult frustration, a fact that would allow Brian's avoidance of his own troubles that much more space to flourish.

The denouement of our relationship was ultimately as revealing as it was brutal and ghastly. One confessional phone call, and that was that. Neither of us ever attempted to figure out what had happened; we never considered that his indiscretion was some result of our own increasing intimacy. We instantly became like the Three Stooges, bumbling along and assuming that appearances were reality. He had slept with someone else, and so our union was defunct. End of story. We had exactly one more conversation in which I cried and he cried, and then we hung up the phone and never spoke to each other again.

The abrupt conclusion of this relationship was, in fact, a perfect metaphor for the relationship itself. Brian and I were, to each other, like the plastic cutout figures in the children's game Colorforms. Each was, to the other, that flat, that malleable, that objectified. Given what each of us wanted—diversion, fantasy, romance without any true involvement—we were extremely well served by the long-distance nature of our coupling. I wanted tenderness, a creative man who could express his feelings and understand mine; he wanted access to the youthful optimism that he had felt leak out of him like air from a punctured tire. That neither of us was prepared for genuine intimacy is clear from the way that we released a supposedly serious coupling like children would let go of their balloons. I'm not suggesting that this particular relationship was meant to be—in retrospect, I see that Brian and I were shockingly unsuited—but it is clear that his indiscretion could easily have been regarded as a momentary crisis, the sort of surmountable, manageable conflict that couples face all the time. Yet, significantly, never for a moment did either of us consider that there was any recourse available to us but to say good-bye.

For my part, what these two examples of commitment-phobic men have in common is what they tell me about my own capacity for objectification. On the surface, the two men could not have been more different—corporate versus creative, withholding versus expressive—but in terms of what they could offer me emotionally they might as well have been twins separated at birth. I entered an involvement with each of these men with a preexisting need to be swept away, to find true love—and in the end it was of very little importance to me that their particular wrappings were different.

And the fact is that my very readiness, my unbridled enthusiasm when faced with the possibility of a relationship with either of these men and the vast number of men who cropped up before and after them, reveals the opposite of what it would seem to. I was like a patch of quicksand, and any man who had the misfortune to enter my vicinity was instantly in jeopardy. What I had to offer was not my great ability to love them; I couldn't even see them. The true identity of each man I became involved with could not have been less important to me. Little wonder that the men I got involved with wanted out so quickly. The affection and regard I had to offer had nothing to do with appreciating them and everything to do with my own private, murky, urgent needs.

Had anyone suggested to me years ago that I was very much like the men I routinely became involved with (and these two men in particular), I would have blanched and responded with furious protestations. Such an idea would have been pure blasphemy to me back then. Well, as it turns out, I *was* very much like these men. The only real difference between me and my beaux was that I was content to hand over to them the responsibility (and blame) of keeping my romantic liaisons short and superficial, thus passively evading the demands of intimacy and blithely retaining my ignorance about my true motives. After each relationship burst into flames, I'd examine my ex-partner's behavior with the clarity of hindsight and see quite plainly that all the signs of ruin had been firmly in place. What made my heart race with anticipatory joy was not spying my true Prince Charming, but instead finding a man who was willing to do the dirty work of keeping us both unattached, while I settled in for what to me was a gratifyingly predictable ride.

For all of the ways people of my generation resist the trappings of adulthood—postponing career decisions, waiting until the last possible minute to have children, remaining far too long in studio apartments jammed with our parents' cast-off furniture—the fact is that the cultural climate in which we came of age forced us to confront bleak, existential realities far sooner than earlier generations. I happened to have been fortunate to have had a fairly protected upbringing, and still I occasionally glanced at the news and knew that terrible trouble lay just around the corner. And if the true indicator of adulthood lies in self-acceptance, then it seems we commitment-phobes have found the perfect avoidance tactic. To refuse romantic commitment and the intimacy such involvement affords is to resist—at least in part—exposure to the very self-knowledge that is the essence of the adult self. On the one hand, it's not a bad option—perpetual youth. Adulthood carries lots of pain and difficulty as well as the occasional sacrifice of a fantasy here and there. On the other hand, the alternative to embracing the adult self is a lifetime spent as a snarly adolescent. And as we all know, forty-year-old adolescents don't get invited to many dinner parties.

4

The Second Mrs. de Winter in Spurs

Female Commitment-Phobes and the Media

MANY YEARS AGO, in the early seventies, my oldest sister handed me a thick paperback novel, along with the solemn instruction, "Read this." I glanced at its cover and saw that the book was *Rebecca*, Daphne du Maurier's 1930s classic tale of love and torture from beyond the grave. I remember thinking it odd that my older sister, who was the quintessence of hip in her self-embroidered, low-slung white jeans and purple ribbed T-shirt, who never read a newspaper but cared in her own way about current events (enough to plaster the walls of her bedroom with poignant and colorful anti-war posters), should choose such an old-fashioned book to share with me. However, as soon as I cracked the dusty cover, this paradox was immediately cleared up. In spite of its dated packaging, the story is timeless. Few writers are as gifted as du Maurier at achieving that perfect balance of obsession and supplication that characterizes the romantic romp with an elusive man.

The novel's premise is satisfyingly deceptive. The narrator, who remains unnamed throughout the entire book, is a self-described colorless young woman, desperately insecure and sufficiently down on her luck to be traveling to Monte Carlo as the paid companion to a porcine and obnoxious older woman, Mrs. Van Hopper. Our bashful narrator happens to encounter a man regarded as the catch of the Continent, the wealthy and compelling Maximillian de Winter, who is taking a holiday of his own, presumably in an effort to recover from his recent heartbreak: the early death of his ethereally beautiful young wife, Rebecca. For reasons that our narrator cannot possibly begin to fathom, Maxim de Winter takes her up, whisking her about the gambling paradise in his convertible sports car, keeping her both giddily enthralled and completely baffled. When Mrs. Van Hopper bursts the bubble of our narrator's adventure by informing her of their unexpected and immediate departure, de Winter delivers a shocking retaliative blow—he proposes marriage.

The narrator then does the unthinkable: She marries him, neatly shifting social class and securing fairy-tale romance in one fell swoop. However, things are not as perfect as they seem, a lamentable truth our narrator discovers as soon as she crosses the august threshold of Manderly, de Winter's ancestral estate. From the arctic reception of the staff, the cryptic and not-so-subtly denigrating comments made by his relatives and friends, and the attitude of Maxim himself, who falls into the grimmest of postnuptial moods as soon as the two settle in at his manorial home, our heroine surmises that her battles have just begun. Because, although this unassuming young woman has managed to marry Mr. de Winter, she begins to believe that his devotion will forever elude her. As she sees it, his heart lies wholly entombed with what remains of his first wife, the vibrant and breathtaking and never really dead Rebecca. We, the compassionate readers, follow the protagonist through her agonies of jealousy and self-deprecation, through her awkward pas de deux with the overly critical and apparently still grief-stunned staff. And mostly we follow her through her diligent, if awkward, efforts to read the signals of her remote and mysterious husband.

When I say that the story is deceptive, I'm not speaking of the obvious deception of the narrator by her presumably otherwise-besotted husband. Indeed, by the end of the novel, we come to learn that Maxim is not besotted at all, but rather haunted by his memories of the hex in a party dress to whom he was previously married. What *is* deceptive is du Maurier's manipulation of her readers: She knows we will accept unquestioningly the dynamic of the obsessed but hopelessly inadequate woman grappling with the withheld affections of a more desirable man. Eventually we are permitted to see the real story: It is the narrator's own fixation on Rebecca, her own need for an escape from real intimacy with her husband, that threatens to destroy the fledgling marriage and keeps her occupied, even enthralled, during the majority of the novel's action.

Other than occasional remarks about how distracted, how generally dissatisfied, Maxim seems, most of the narrator's thoughts are engaged in a pointedly rhapsodic and extended meditation on the myriad attributes of her predecessor. The narrator's passion exists not for her husband but for her fantasies concerning her husband's late wife. If he seems depressed, maybe it's because his second wife's got a serious crush, and it's not on him. Little wonder that he spends his days moping about the house, long before Rebecca's corpse is unexpectedly exhumed from the nearby bay—an event that forces him to exchange the role of grieving widower for that of murder suspect.

The second Mrs. de Winter's loony-tunes fixation on anything but her actual relationship suggests a fairly pronounced aversion to intimacy, something that prevents her from fully committing to her husband and her marriage. Not that du Maurier or any of her characters pay this fact the slightest bit of attention. All manner of self-reflection and personality analysis occur in this novel, but the possibility that the narrator's private inclinations might be a significant source of her troubles isn't a point worthy of note. Du Maurier tells it like she sees it: The narrator is a woman consumed by desperate longing for a man who barely deigns to glance her way.

Now, don't get me wrong: I'm demented with love for this

novel. It's utterly sublime. But being obsessed with it doesn't prevent me from seeing that du Maurier's version of this love story conforms most compliantly to the culturally sanctioned model of male-female romantic interaction. Namely, du Maurier is determined to present her female narrator as the hapless, lovesick idolater whose singular goal is winning her husband's fugitive affection, while portraying Maxim, her husband, as an ambivalent, largely disengaged object of desire. And yet, by the novel's conclusion, it's become undeniably clear that he is anything but indifferent; he's hopelessly enamored of his second wife and obsessed with worry that, as she comes to know him more fully, her good feelings for him will disappear. While the narrator's reluctance to take the intimacy plunge—a plunge absolutely essential to the ultimate success or failure of her matrimonial experience—remains unacknowledged by the book's author and main character alike, readers are likely to miss the point altogether that the future of the de Winters' marriage lies not in the masterful hands of Maxim but rather in the delicate mitts of his young and blushing bride.

But the truth is that we enthusiastic partakers of the media's bounty are often meant to miss the point. Because, when it comes to shaping the attitudes of its citizens, one of the culture's most effective tools is the media. Books, movies, television, and, of course, advertising work to reinforce the whole gamut of opinions and assumptions that guide our culture.

Many of these assumptions, regardless of their truth or falsity, are relatively benign. It's practically impossible to turn on the television, for example, without being bombarded by the dairy industry's dispatches regarding the supreme healthfulness of milk. And even though everybody knows that our bodies can barely digest milk, and worse, that our indulgence in even an occasional pint of the stuff sends us hurtling through the cellulite turnstile, it's hard not to feel rather cheerful about milk's wholesome properties as we watch the creamy white beverage cascading into tall glasses.

Unfortunately, the media seem equally willing to reinforce innocent assumptions as they are to reinforce those that are not so innocent. The media's representation of the standard romantic dynamic between men and women, for instance, seems like a pretty willful exercise in the abasement of women and the aggrandizement of men. Here's the culture's preferred version of modern romance: So driven are women to get hitched that they'll stoop to any means necessary to achieve their conjugal goals. Which means that men had better watch it or else they'll end up straitjacketed in some ill-fitting tuxedo, repeating the dread marriage vows like some new breed of ring-bearing chimpanzee.

No matter how complicated the reality of our romantic comings-together might be, the culture—and the media, as facilitators of its message—clings tenaciously to this cartoon version of predator and prey. Even in those rare cases where female romantic ambivalence forces itself into the picture, it's either ignored or explained away as a freakish aberration.

This isn't an accident. The media's depiction of the dynamic between men and women serves a crucial social function. It reassures us that no matter how much the things of this world may change, we can count on certain important suppositions to remain constant. And particularly important to a male-dominated culture is proof of the righteousness of such domination. It's the comfort of logical conclusion, of cause and effect: Men are always more desirable, sought after, valued. No self-respecting patriarchy is going to sacrifice the mythicized image of a woman sitting forlornly by her telephone, chewing her manicured fingernails, and waiting for a phone call from the man of her dreams. It's a portrait that justifies male dominance and female suppliancy, and in its absence, we might be moved to question the legitimacy of this time-honored arrangement.

Clearly, as there's so much riding on the preservation of our perception of female predator and male prey, the possibility of female commitment anxiety can be enormously threatening. Even the slightest suggestion that women might harbor ambivalence or hesitation about committing to a relationship is disturbingly subversive. Fortunately, as a society, we've come up with an ingenious method of dealing with this: We ignore or deny the possibility that women fear commitment. We construct alternative narratives to explain women's reluctance to get romantically involved: They're insane or impossibly arrogant or just plain stupid. Even when a woman's commitment anxiety is fairly obvious, as in the case of the narrator of *Rebecca*, it is presented in such a misleading manner that we're likely to miss it altogether.

Of course, female commitment-phobes do exist in hordes, but don't expect any confirmation of this fact from the media (with the possible exception of the enchanting movie *Miami Rhapsody*—a true groundbreaker in its unapologetic portrayal of Sarah Jessica Parker's character as a dyed-in-the-wool commitment-phobe). The fact is that the elaborate machinations that the female half of the population undertakes in order to evade commitment is an exceedingly prevalent—and almost universally ignored—theme in most forms of popular entertainment. But because the mainstream media's job is to protect the status quo, which in the case of this discussion means that television and movies and commercial fiction do whatever they can to reinforce the notion that the reluctant half of any couple is necessarily going to be the man, the media's preferred treatment of female commitment phobia is not to explore it but to exploit it.

Lest you think that my criticism of the media means that I am not a fan, perhaps I should offer some clarification. I'm a junkie, though my walk on the wild side doesn't take me anywhere near as swank as the Viper Room. I'm addicted to mass media, junk entertainment, the more diversionary and mindlessly superficial, the better. Friends call to read me passages of the latest translation of

Dante's *Inferno* and, yes, I'll agree that what I'm listening to is beautiful, transcendent, but they know and I know that I'm waiting to release the mute button and get back to *Hard Copy*.

(And, now that I've revealed myself in all my true, *People*-magazine sensibility, I should add that the examples I reflect on in this chapter are in no way meant to be comprehensive. The books or television shows or movies I discuss here are simply those of which I've joyously partaken; I'm certain other examples will spring to mind as you read this. And by all means feel free to fill in the blanks and add your own examples to the limited survey I've provided. We're friends, after all. And, what's more, I plan to drop by your place for drinks in the very near future.)

Having exposed myself as a bona fide media zombie, any criticism of my personal electronic deity may seem mighty strange — biting the hand that feeds me, so to speak. However, as one who's spent the majority of her waking hours deep in the media's thrall, I have had ample opportunity to observe something of the manner in which it reduces the complicated relations between the sexes into a rigidly prescribed and laughably oversimplified blueprint of god and disciple. Whether overtly stated, as in the case of Jeannie's pet name, "master," for Major Anthony Nelson in the sixties television classic *I Dream of Jeannie*, or more subtly expressed, as with the marveling moon-eyes Dana Scully makes at Fox "Spooky" Mulder each week on the current cult favorite, *The X Files*, the distinction between adorer and adored remains plenty clear.

According to this blueprint, even the most independent, apparently self-sufficient woman would happily chuck it all for the chance to register for KitchenAid appliances and flatware at Bloomingdale's. And yet, scratch the surface of any of these alleged manhunters and, as often as not, what you'll find is a commitment-phobe, one who — being female — has next to no understanding of or context for her conflicting desires and behavior.

So why is it that we can't make the distinction, whether on

the television screen or in our own true lives, between a woman madly flailing about for a man and one who'd rather peel off her skin with a paring knife than land a husband? Maybe all those bad-tempered critics of television were right when they insisted that eighteen or twenty hours a day of childhood TV viewing would turn us into drooling chowderheads, because we, the audience, both male and female, habitually forget to question whether the assumptions about our romantic dynamic depicted on the television screen bear much relationship at all to our actual experiences in love's trenches.

We don't question; we settle in on the couch with our nachos and our light beer and we smile as our brain waves grow as flat as the horizon. We chuckle (*Cybill*) or grow maudlin and teary (*Sisters*) as we observe the exaggerated and often desperate efforts of women on the quest for the holy grail of romantic validation. Along the way, male viewers are reminded of their overwhelming desirability and adulation, and females are shown that whatever their goals or achievements, when it comes to the manhunt, everything else falls by the wayside. Because women, at least on television or in the movies, are eminently distractible when a carrot in the form of an attractive man is dangled before their noses.

What we are not encouraged to do is to take issue with the one-dimensionality of these portrayals. Because the creators and the viewers are acting on this common assumption—that women want to get married and have babies—even when the signals suggest the absolute opposite, the assumption holds strong. Consider Mary Tyler Moore, a.k.a. Mary Richards, that seventies television folk hero, everybody's angel. We worried about Mary in her adorable studio apartment, polishing her wooden M while the cold Minneapolis night raged outside those French doors. The absence of a partner in this lovely young woman's life was mysterious and troubling. Where were all the single men? Never mind that Mary herself, as the first female news producer at her television station, was forging new professional territory, we worried (because we were expected to) that however content Ms. Richards might seem in her cheerfully decorated and self-contained domicile, time was marching on and there was a conspicuous absence of wedding showers on the horizon.

That Mary Richards was obviously ambivalent about making a commitment to a relationship, that she struggled with her fears about giving up her independence and professional focus—so much so that in the course of that very lengthy series she never really had what would be considered a serious boyfriend—was plainly beside the point. Mary's defining characteristic was not her competence or her charm but her singleness. And if she didn't know enough to obsess about it, then by God, we were more than happy to do it for her.

But the truth is that Mary paid a price for her romantic ambivalence, however unacknowledged it remained. Her tense, occasionally brittle asexuality was no accident; rather, her demeanor was a case of personality as explanation. She was the perpetual prepubescent, pristine as the virgin many viewers likely suspected she was. This way, Mary's solitude seemed not the result of reluctance or an unwillingness to compromise, but rather an appropriate state for one of her stalled psychosexual development. A prepubescent, but with excellent breasts. Nothing wrong with that, right?

Acting as an obvious foil to Mary was her sensual and disorderly—and routinely excoriated—upstairs neighbor, Rhoda Morgenstern. Rhoda was another story entirely: creative, smart-mouthed, experienced. Disobedience rippled just beneath her surface, compelling the show's creators to punish her with a parade of ever-changing scarf headwear and exile to the attic apartment. Rhoda worried about her weight (and who wouldn't, living upstairs from that Popsicle stick in a pant suit), she worried about her looks (ditto), she worried about the fact that her apartment had no interior doors. Rhoda, with her love-bead room dividers and her career as a department store window dresser, was a different sort of cautionary tale: Unlike Mary, she was acutely aware of the disaster that was her own single status. Her problem was not that she didn't recognize her predicament, but rather that she hadn't learned to control her unfeminine impulses sufficiently to solve it. Edgy and outspoken, too street-smart for her own good, Rhoda's strong will would be—apparently had been— enough to turn off any man.

Unlike her downstairs neighbor, Rhoda accepted the fact that a woman's ultimate dream involved a slow stroll down the aisle. What she did not realize, though the show's producers evidently did, was that until she learned to behave herself, such happiness would continue to elude her. Unlike Mary, Rhoda gave full voice to her feelings of loneliness and romantic longing, though somehow she made even these typically virtuous sentiments seem like expressions of an unbridled appetite. If one of the purposes of *The Mary Tyler Moore Show* was to defuse a potentially threatening career gal like Mary—ostensibly by revealing her hand-wringing at dinner parties, for which she had (symbolism being what it will) less than enough food to serve, or whining plaintively to her boss ("Mr. Grant!"), less overtly by completely desexualizing her—Rhoda was an example of a woman who, because of her fundamental seditiousness, won no favor at all. Even when she got her own show, *Rhoda*, and married the wondrous Joe, they wouldn't leave her alone, ignominiously forcing her into divorce court even before her wedding dress could be properly dry-cleaned and preserved.

By the mid-eighties, the less-than-perceptive television viewer might have imagined that the climate had changed regarding the portrayal of women on the small screen. Of course, the more shrewd television aficionado knew better. It was around this time that the country was swept by *Cheers* fever. *Cheers* chronicled the misadventures of Sam Malone, confirmed ladies' man, former ball player, recovering alcoholic, and, as the show begins, new proprietor of a popular saloon in the heart of hard-drinking Boston. Soon enough we got to know the bar's regular customers, a decidedly quirky and eccentric group. In the early days, one of the establishment's more colorful characters was the waitress Diane. Diane is the perfect object for a television writer's derision: She's a woman and she's way too big for her britches. Diane is a frustrated intellectual, a student of psychology, and, as we soon learn, a patient of this discipline as well. Sam and Diane soon commence what will become a complicated, on-again-off-again relationship extending over many antic-filled years.

Now, Sam Malone is a true commitment-phobe: handsome and suave, pathologically flirtatious, always interested but impossible to get. Diane, on the other hand, is a patent lunatic. And yet, in spite of their myriad differences concerning everything from sensibility to education, the attraction between Sam and Diane just won't die. This is probably because Diane is in many ways exactly like Sam—she's attractive, she's cocky, she's indecisive—and yet the same characteristics that make Sam so irresistible leave Diane a sitting duck for the audience's contempt. Though it is perfectly clear that theirs is a mutual game of approach and avoidance, we are given to understand with absolutely no evidence at all that Sam is the true ambivalent and that, given any indication that he is finally ready to make a real commitment, all of Diane's indecision would evaporate, leaving her sprinting for the altar. By deliberately undermining Diane's credibility with the apparently shocking revelation that she's spent some time on a therapist's couch, and by allowing her to personify that most laughable of specimens, the arrogant woman, *Cheers* managed to position two identically inclined commitment-phobes on opposite sides of the spectrum: Sam, sane and selective; Diane, desperate to commit and inspiring the desperate desire in others to see her committed, preferably to some loony bin lock-up and for good.

When a show does make an effort to realistically represent relationship fears and ambivalences, said show often falls prey to the dreaded fate of bad ratings. During the mid-eighties another show was born, a gem of a show that drew a far more modest audience than *Cheers*, in spite of its delectable brilliance. This was *The Days and Nights of Molly Dodd*, a sort of Reagan-era stepsister of *The Mary Tyler Moore Show* and *That Girl* that chronicled the life of a young career woman, the eponymous Molly, in exhilarating Manhattan. (The program is probably syndicated now on Lifetime Television, or would be if the executives there really cared about the female viewership they claim to serve.)

In any event, Molly was played by the peerless Blair Brown in all her spirited, redheaded splendor, and I spent many a night sitting with my best friend on her itchy brown plaid couch (named, by her, Dirty Burlap), alternately sympathizing with and envying Molly's adventures. We loved Molly's apartment—a sprawling and charmingly appointed Upper West Side aerie whose rent, in reality, only Christina Onassis could afford, yet resourceful Molly somehow managed to keep things afloat on her salary as a bookstore clerk. Such was the stuff of our fantasies: a chic but eccentric wardrobe, a workplace that attracted interesting, literate men, a dinner-party friendly home. Hello, New Jerusalem.

The truth was that Molly had had her share of troubles, including an early and disastrous marriage to the devastatingly attractive but hopelessly unreliable Fred, a jazz musician (if you want to talk about badly conceived plans). As the show begins, Molly has just reluctantly divorced Fred and found herself thrust into the New York singles scene—which is, at its best, an arbitrary and baffling universe.

Given the show's great promise, it's difficult not to wonder whether the rapid demise of *The Days and Nights of Molly Dodd* was a result of the fact that Molly steadfastly refused to be demeaned by her status as an unattached woman in her middle thirties. While the show's writers clearly delighted in portraying all of the unspeakable humiliations Molly endured at the hands of commitment-shy men and the agonies of doubt she suffered wondering if she would ever find a man capable of sustaining that dual challenge of being both exciting and responsible, the program managed to communicate something more than just the hilarity of female romantic desperation. Molly Dodd was engaged in a serious, fearless, even gallant quest for self-discovery. As much as she desired love, she also valued her independence and was fiercely determined to resist the temptation of once again placing the responsibility for her own happiness and satisfaction in a man's hands. Hers was the struggle, throughout the course of the show, to know herself, to find contentment on her own terms—and as a result she was just as frequently unavailable for real romantic engagement as the men on whom the show resolutely focused its spotlight.

In the context of the media, fictional characters are not the only ones susceptible to biased and inaccurate representation. Take television talk shows, for example, programs that have long occupied a special place in the hearts of television freaks. If you're an old crone like me, you probably remember the early days of Dinah Shore and Mike Douglas eliciting madcap comments from such celebrity guests as Burt Reynolds and Mason Reese, but those days are long gone. They vanished the moment Oprah Winfrey burst onto daytime programming, making girlfriendliness and intimate public confessions seem positively irresistible. Oprah was followed in quick succession by a battalion of crowd-taming moderators—from Ricki Lake to Jenny Jones to Montel Williams—all possessors of the ability to make ordinary people sit on televised sound stages and reveal experiences of a profoundly private nature.

While the producers of these raucous talk shows seem pleased to address any issue with a personal bent, they are most drawn to topics concerning love. Or, I should say, concerning love troubles. The liveliest and most heart-wrenching of these shows are those that focus on women who have been consistently wronged by the men in their lives; women who have been impregnated and abandoned; women who have discovered or been confronted with their partner's infidelity, as often as not involving a family member or close friend of the wronged woman; women who are habitually physically or psychologically abused by their spouses.

Everyone—the studio audience, the hosts, the television viewers (which must include all of us, given the remarkable ratings these shows enjoy)—is moved by these sorrowful tales of heartache and betrayal. Everyone is shocked at the barbarism of the men who wreak such unconscionable havoc. Everyone except the inveterate crank of a viewer unwilling to regard the women onstage as powerless and innocent adult-sized children. Because, if you don't accept that these women are absolutely helpless, you're forced to wonder what exactly is in it for all of these maidens weeping piteously upon the stage. What precisely are they doing with these partners who make them so unhappy? Did the fairy godmother of free will simply skip over these women?

Now, I'm as sympathetic as the next person to legitimate issues like Battered Woman Syndrome and chronic poverty, but if you've ever seen one of these programs, you know that lots of the women telling their sorry tales fall into a less dire category—they're grooving on heartache. Television talk shows, amusing and cathartic though they can be, rarely challenge the notion of female as hapless, masochistic victim. But if you watch the women on these shows, the ones involved in the damaging or unsatisfying or futureless relationships, what you really notice is the ferocity with which many of them attempt to defend their self-destructive choices. They aren't interested in surrender, however much they might enjoy the chance to complain about their various hardships to an audience of sympathetic listeners. Never is it suggested to either these women or their audience that their deliberate pursuit of doomed-to-fail relationships might be an indirect way of guaranteeing that they'll never have to follow through with an equal, genuinely intimate relationship. It's easier to be a victim, because when you're a victim, the whole notion of making difficult decisions and taking responsibility for your life is moot.

Just as television has continually metamorphosed to keep abreast of social evolution, so have movies. However, no matter how much movies have adapted to cultural change—replacing, for example, the once-popular musicals' elegant dance numbers with extended sequences featuring raw sexual encounters and full frontal nudity—the quest for love (and the difficulties therein) remains a favorite topic for moviemakers and moviegoers alike. Where we once had Bette Davis receiving a lighted cigarette from her lover rather than a kiss (in what was probably the celluloid pinnacle of thwarted romance, *Now, Voyager*), we are now treated to Demi Moore committing corporate date-rape of Michael Douglas. Some call it progress.

Although romantic comedy seems to have surpassed romantic dramas in the affection of the contemporary movie audience, the lovelorn female, whatever the genre, has always enjoyed a secure place in American cinema. And just as the commitment issue has ballooned in our actual lives, it has also managed to weasel into the favored subject matter of Hollywood's current writers and directors.

Unlike television series, which are required to come up with a compelling problem and repeat it over and over each week, in movies, quite the opposite is true: Resolution is everything. However true to life or absurd the action on the screen, by the time two hours are up, everything sorts itself out. The movie audience is aware of this necessity; indeed, we'd be bereft and demanding our money back if the credits started rolling without a trumpeting, against-all-odds, emotionally resolved conclusion. Movie studios are fueled far more by box office hopes than by a desire to offer us a realistic representation of our own experiences. We don't go to the movies to see real-life relationships with their relentless patterns and frequent total absence of closure, we go to see montage sequences of Julia Roberts modeling oversized picture hats.

Meg Ryan has always been a sort of picture-hat favorite, an

exceedingly cooperative and cheerful representative of the female gender, as the viewers of her nineties hit *Sleepless in Seattle* can attest. In this particular picture, Ryan plays a hopeless romantic, a woman obsessed by the idea that there exists a singular soulmate intended only for her, and all she has to do is hold tight and wait for him to materialize. When the movie opens, she's engaged to a man she's fears is not The One, and so when she has occasion, during a late-night radio broadcast, to hear Tom Hanks's character wax rhapsodic about his beloved but tragically deceased spouse, Ryan becomes convinced that this faraway, unseen man is her sentimental equal.

Ryan's character's fiancé seems literally to evaporate from her memory as she sets off across the nation on her quest for Mr. Right. And in spite of a series of Laurel-and-Hardian mishaps and crossed signals, by the time the movie concludes, Ryan has managed to pull off the most improbable feat of securing widower Hanks for her very own. Now, wasn't I saying something earlier about trumpeting, against-all-odds movie conclusions?

It's certainly lovely that we all got to exit the theater imagining tow-headed Ryan lending a woman's touch to Hank's enviably located and very smartly turned-out two-story waterfront house. But you know and I know that if cinema had any desire to tell the real story, they'd be forced to show Meg Ryan's character twenty years from now, still hunched in front of her clock radio, listening to late-night talk shows and indulging in PMS weepiness while polishing off her third still-frozen Sara Lee pound cake. Let's just say that Ryan's character was extremely fortunate to have her fate placed in the hands of Hollywood's rigidly benevolent screenwriters, because otherwise she would have been slotted to live out her days as a compulsive fantasy hound, kept perfectly static and isolated by her preference for dreamed-up romantic perfection, rather than its real, and sometimes awfully messy, counterpart.

Modern moviemakers are very fond of exploring the prickly contretemps of women in heated pursuit of openly unavailable men.

More often than not, the plots of these films play out in a way that reinforces two culturally sanctified assumptions about the male-female dynamic. On the one hand, the depiction of a woman jumping through hoops in order to attract the attention of a man whose interests lie elsewhere reminds viewers that men are creatures of such desirability and value that women are rendered powerless in their presence, regardless of how unlikely the chances that these feelings of adulation will be the returned by men inspiring them. Remember Mary Stuart Masterson's pixieish character in *Some Kind of Wonderful* reinventing despair as her crush on the character played by Eric Stoltz remained unrequited until the film's final moments? Or love-crazed Bridget Fonda's character in *Singles*, and her mortifying efforts to secure the Pleistocene affections of the rocker-boy played by Matt Dillon? It's all in a day's work at the humiliation factory, ladies. Now, don't forget to punch the time clock.

On the other hand, portraying women in the position of being overtaken by uncontrollable desire gives filmmakers the opportunity to distinguish between acceptable and unacceptable female behavior. Most women, having received the usual amount of social training, are content to worship from afar, and if they do break down and indulge in some active pursuit, they manage to express their romantic interest cautiously, indirectly, with calculated discretion.

Think of Miss Kenton (Emma Thompson), for example, suppressing her romantic urges for a stonily implacable Stevens (Anthony Hopkins) in *Remains of the Day*, that heart-wrenching study of mixed messages, thwarted desire, and cruelly beautiful architecture in post–World War II England. Or Fiona (Kristin Scott Thomas) in *Four Weddings and a Funeral*, concealing until the very last minute her desperate love for Charles (Hugh Grant), a character whose terror of commitment is so outsized and consuming it manages to inspire an entire movie plot. Fiona's confession sets a new standard in self-effacing, sardonic deference (a performance enhanced by her dry, almost brittle English wit); she reveals her feelings so regretfully that it becomes practically a point of honor for Charles to demur, so as not to disappoint her expectation of rejection. The self-denigrating reserve of Thompson's and Scott Thomas's characters (both British—coincidence or fate?) offers female audiences a useful blueprint for the manner in which decent, upstanding women should behave, even in the face of great emotional distress.

The flip side of the coin—the female anti–role models—provides a sort of cautionary tale for male and female viewers alike. Who could ever forget Alex Forrest (played by Glenn Close) being both drowned and shot in that seminal eighties backlash movie, *Fatal Attraction*—one of cinema's most alarming depictions of a woman driving herself crazy over an unavailable man. When Alex sleeps with Dan Gallagher (played by Michael Douglas), a happily though slightly bored married man, Dan considers the encounter a one-shot deal. Alex does not. As Dan, at first gently and later more forcefully, attempts to clarify the misunderstanding, Alex grows increasingly determined to win him.

During the course of the narrative, Alex transforms from an ordinary if frustrated woman into a murderous sociopath. Because of this, it's easy to forget that before her metamorphosis Alex is a classic example of a commitment-phobe, setting her sights on a pretty clearly unavailable man and unwilling to deal directly with the disappointment she feels when he refuses to become further involved with her. The more rejecting Dan becomes, the more frantic Alex is to change his mind. She is completely out of touch with the concept of cause and effect: Somebody says no, you make tracks—and not because you're a loser, but because what would be the point of wasting your valuable time and energy on an emotional entanglement that's very likely to make you miserable?

Much has been written about the fact that the creators of *Fatal Attraction* were compelled to make some last-minute changes before the film's official release. In what has become common practice—

a sort of systematized failure of nerve wherein executives elicit the reaction of Joe America while artistic changes are still possible — the movie was screened for preview audiences with its original ending: Alex's despair drives her to commit suicide, but in such a way that she implicates Dan in her death. What these executives did not anticipate was that audiences would be so outraged at Alex's behavior (her refusal to meekly accept Dan's dismissive treatment) that they would find intolerable anything but the savage butchering of Close's character. Bear in mind that this audience included both men *and* women, a fact that illustrates the complicity of both genders in demanding a particular standard of behavior from females. In what is quite plainly an archetypal reenactment of dragon slaying, Dan and his good wife, Beth (Anne Archer), join forces at the movie's revised conclusion and literally kill the beast, demonstrating exactly what happens to women who don't know their place.

Of course, not all movies follow these rigid guidelines; some do attempt to subvert the culturally sanctioned party line. Sometimes filmmakers allow a female character to break the rules, but they insist that she be appropriately punished for doing so. This was the case with the movie *The Piano*, in which Ada (played by Holly Hunter) taught us a thing or two about the disposability of dialogue. Hunter's character, a willful and determined mail-order bride who rejects the relative convenience of the spoken word, traverses a staggering distance to the wilds of eighteenth-century New Zealand with her precocious daughter-translator in tow, only to find that the man to whom she's betrothed (Stewart, played by the usually adorable Sam Neill) is an exceedingly irritating stick.

But far more distressing than her presumed romantic disappointment is the fact that her beloved and greatly schlepped piano has proved impossible to transport through the vegetation-dense and emphatically unpaved New Zealand brush. For Ada, a voluntary mute, her piano represents far more than a vehicle for show tunes; Ada's piano, which she plays with an exquisite erotic intensity, is the externalized symbol and literal conduit of all her profoundly passionate impulses. In fact, it is only when Stewart insists that they abandon the piano, which he regards as the height of frivolity, that Ada withdraws definitively from him, letting the marriage die before it even begins.

Meanwhile another local man, Baines (played by the snarlingly sexy Harvey Keitel, who proves once and for all that one should never underestimate a man with love handles), apparently undaunted by logistical difficulties, takes possession of the instrument. Intrigued by Ada, he devises a plan whereby she can buy back the piano with the currency of her naked body. It doesn't take long before Ada falls wildly in love with a wholly reciprocating Baines, but so strong is her resistance to the very notion of romantic intimacy—an intimacy that she has plainly spent her entire life avoiding, restricting its highly charged expression to her piano playing—that she refuses to admit even to herself the true nature of her feelings. Baines seems to understand that Ada needs to be distracted from the powerful connection between them if it is to be allowed to flourish, and so relies on the bartering subterfuge to ensure his access to her.

Because Ada so obviously adheres to her own ethical course, it's clear that her reluctance to become involved has very little to do with the violation of her marriage contract, a contract that was broken beyond repair in her eyes by her husband's early betrayal. Moreover, it seems that Ada recognizes that Baines's intensity and individualistic integrity are equal to her own, and so any genuine contact with him would threaten to violate the solitude she's so invested in protecting.

Eventually Stewart becomes aware of the relationship between Baines and his wife, and after a dramatic and violent confrontation, the lovers, as they have gradually become, are free to take their leave. So powerful is Ada's fear of the sustained intimate involvement she anticipates with Baines that she impulsively attempts to drown herself during ocean passage to their new shared home. Although

Ada decides at the last minute to save herself, the image of her fully clad body plunging determinedly underwater tied to the leg of her piano not only tells us something of the ways in which clinging to our old, once-useful defenses can ultimately destroy us, but also speaks evocatively of the lengths to which some women will go to ensure their independence.

On rare occasions, women are allowed to challenge or break cultural rules without sustaining potentially mortal injury. For example, Paul Mazursky's 1970s homage to the transforming power of the women's movement, *An Unmarried Woman*, both acknowledges its female lead's reluctance to make a commitment and manages to refrain from riddling her torso with semiautomatic bullets. In this film, Erica (played by Jill Clayburgh, in all her braless, clingy T-shirted splendor) struggles to piece her life back together after the unexpected and brutal defection of her longtime spouse. Through filmy, soft-focus lens, we watch Erica's shell-shocked but game efforts to develop an identity other than that of wife. Set in Manhattan, the film is a delicious artifact of the 1970s, trailing Erica to her labor-free job at a Soho art gallery, to warm and supportive consciousness-raising sessions with wry women friends, to appointments with her wonderfully soothing therapist, Tanya, who wears turquoise and silver amulets, sits Indian-style on the floor during sessions, and relies on such phrases as, "Turn off the guilt." It's the ideal movie to watch when you're curled up in bed with a rotten cold or debilitating cramps.

In any event, Erica eventually meets a mesmerizing and sexy abstract expressionist painter (played by Alan Bates) who falls wildly in love with her. All goes swimmingly for a while, what with Erica continuing to evolve personally while at the same time seeing some excellent action—that is until Bates's character begins to indulge in some bad habits. Namely, he starts to assume that his work is more important than hers, which, given that he's a famous and fabulously wealthy artist and her work seems to involve standing around a flatteringly lit gallery space looking thin, it arguably is. But this is not the point, as Erica firmly points out. Even if she made her living (or rather supplemented her generous alimony checks) as a street cleaner or compulsive hand-washer, her pursuits would necessarily be as valuable as anyone else's, even if that anyone is the next Jackson Pollock (he's not, something that becomes instantly clear upon one's first sighting of those goofy oversized canvases).

The situation reaches a climax when Bates's character insists that Erica join him for the summer in bucolic Vermont and Erica holds her ground (a mystifying decision, if you've ever attempted to survive August in New York City, when the odor of steamy sidewalk urine hits a peak of ripeness), declining, for at least that particular moment, to resume a life in which she plays only a supporting role. And, gratifyingly, Erica is not made to pay any hideous price for her insubordination, strolling jauntily away from her adoring painter as the movie credits roll. We know they'll be reunited once summer's over, and in the meantime Erica will be content knowing that she's been successful in her self-assertion.

Films such as *An Unmarried Woman* that acknowledge the considerable compromises committed relationships require from women, and the ambivalence with which we consequently approach them, are the exception. In novels, however, this type of exploration is more common. This is likely because such a large percentage of a novel's content consists of interior thoughts on the part of the narrator or characters, thus there's more freedom to be nonconformist or express honest, rather than predigested and prettied-up, emotion. There's no punishment for thinking or feeling things that are publicly unacceptable, because if one is careful, these thoughts or emotions can remain private. Of course, the fact that books don't cost $40 million to produce and are not reliant on the enthusiasm of the viewing public for the recoupment of those dollars might have some impact on the relative creative independence of novelists. But, once again, I digress.

And this is not to say, in any event, that all novels resist the temptation to reinforce the culturally approved interpretation of male-female relationships, wherein the woman is always eagerly and at any cost pursuing commitment. Even when female characters go to extreme means to avoid the security or contentment of marriage, or bridle at the restrictions of the marriages they're in, it's surprisingly easy to attribute their actions or attitudes to something other than a disinclination to entertain or fully enter a committed relationship.

Isabel Moore, the narrator of Mary Gordon's beautiful and moving novel *Final Payments*, is considered many things: a dutiful daughter, a saint, a martyr. When Isabel is twenty years old, her elderly father suffers a debilitating stroke and she decides that it is her singlehanded responsibility to care for him. For the next eleven years, her life essentially stands still as her close friends move on to careers, marriages, and families. Although she was a gifted and ambitious college student before her father's illness struck, she abandons all her plans and devotes herself to sustaining her father and his household.

When her father finally dies, Isabel is at the same time stricken with grief and exhilarated by the relief of having the possibilities of her life restored to her. She decides to move from Queens to upstate New York, to be close to her friend Liz and to begin a job arranged for her by Liz's local politician husband, John. Thrilling to her new freedom, Isabel finds an apartment, begins this first job of her adult life, and fantasizes about romantic involvement. The first romantic situation she finds herself in, however, is not the one of her fantasies: She drunkenly goes to bed with Liz's husband, a man for whom both she and Liz primarily feel contempt. This act provokes many reactions: Liz's criticism, which threatens to jeopardize a lifelong friendship; Isabel's own sense of extreme shame; John's unsurprising assumption that the professional relationship between them is now also a sexual one.

And Isabel doesn't stop there. If her first lover after years of celibacy is married to her closest friend and is a man she could never care for, her second lover seems to be equally unsuitable— Liz's best friend, Hugh, also married, with a possessive wife and a history of philandering. Because Hugh is an undeniably appealing man—attractive, intelligent, complex—and because Isabel's longing for him, in all his unavailability, is so powerful, it's easy simply to get caught up in her desire to win Hugh. Isabel sees herself as the pursuer, and we are happy to oblige her perception.

But were the reader to look at the whole picture—to consider the eleven years of voluntary and complete isolation, the first affair with a man who, by virtue of his marriage to Isabel's friend and his general unpleasantness, is an utterly inappropriate choice, and finally her more substantial involvement with a man whom every single woman has been trying to pry from his wife's tenacious grip for years—it suggests that Isabel may be approaching her romantic life from the vantage point of a serious commitment-phobe.

Because Isabel is the kind of person every woman would want to have as a friend—funny, sarcastic, genuinely caring—it is with real pleasure that we observe her progression toward a happier and more satisfying emotional life. This progress does not occur, however, until she endures the kind of overwhelming crisis that demands an honest reevaluation of the hidden feelings and impulses that are propelling her into unsuitable relationships and situations. It is not until she is forced into a more honest relationship with herself—one that acknowledges pain and anger, as well as love and devotion—that she is prepared to engage in a real relationship with a partner.

Often in fiction, as in life, it is only after a period of personal crisis that a woman is able to confront her commitment phobia. The intense despair and introspection that accompany catastrophe can result in the sort of increased self-knowledge that reveals what our shrinks are so frantic to prove to us: The compensating defenses we've developed are ultimately more damaging than the initial injury they sprang up in response to. In *Rebecca* (which by now, I trust, you've all raced out to buy and are breathlessly reading), the narrator's world virtually has to crumble before she is willing to risk a closer relationship with herself and, through this, a closer relationship with her husband. During the couple's "honeymoon" phase, before Maxim is accused of his late wife's murder, the narrator has already come close to effectively destroying what appeared to be her life's single miracle—the possibility of love with a man whom she respects and admires. And it is only when the brutal forces of the outside world encroach that the narrator is compelled to turn her focus away from the seductive thoughts of Maxim's first wife and onto her husband himself, a man whose miserable isolation has only been exaggerated by the fact that his wife, for the majority of the novel, has so completely misread him. And had Rebecca's body remained entombed underwater, had its accidental discovery not set this novel on a different and unexpected course, one wonders whether the narrator might ever have had the will to release her own hold on Rebecca's memory and return to the living world, where in order for a marriage to work, intimacies both physical and emotional and commitment to one's partner are required.

Rebecca illustrates especially well the deceptive influence of our assumptions regarding the power balance between men and women. Yes, the narrator plainly sees herself as the less desirable partner in the marriage: She's not glamorous or exceptionally beautiful, nor is she as cultured as her spouse, coming as she does from a class lower than the one into which she marries. And we readers are so familiar with and fond of this fantasy scenario—exceedingly fortunate Plain Jane subverts logic and fate by winning the fabulous prince—that we never think to question its veracity or to imagine the same story from any other perspective. So accepting are we of the exceedingly lucky ugly duckling narrative (so envious, perhaps?) that we never consider that the celebrated Mr. de Winter felt just as fortunate as his bride, though for markedly different reasons. The narrator is youthful and innocent, unmanipulative, and possessed of an intransigent sweetness and modesty. Her enthusiasm and easy joy make her a pleasure to be around, certainly for the reader and presumably for her husband. So, why do we simply accept at face value the narrator's own sense of profound unworthiness?

Because if you're told a particular story over and over again, and in countless different media, it begins to take on the weight of truth. Cultural mythology is like this: Enough people express a given idea, and all of a sudden it's as though the idea has always existed, unassailable and right. Witness the fact that more than fifty years after *Rebecca* was published (and turned, by Alfred Hitchcock, into a brilliant film), we blithely accept the nearly identical scenario in Garry Marshall's *Pretty Woman*, a film that would like us to accept with a straight face that Richard Gere is the romantic catch and Julia Roberts (the dictionary's and God's definition of natural beauty), the beneficiary of extreme good luck.

Back when the social tenets were arranged in such a way that women were absolutely dependent on men for both economic survival and social legitimacy, men really were pursued with vigor by women because forming a partnership might be the difference between a contented or a miserable existence. But as women have accepted the privilege and the burden of our own autonomy, the myth of the desirable and sought-after man not only has become obsolete, its continuing acceptance by women has worked to significantly undermine our progress toward the role of equal partner. Which leaves us in the losing position of having to both slave away at our jobs during the week *and* worry about whether some Romeo will deign to ask us out once the weekend rolls around.

PART 2

Profiles

All names and identifying characteristics have been changed to protect the commitment-phobic. This is a book, not a kamikaze mission.

5

Jesus Wept

The Lure of the
Unavailable Man

FOR A COMMITMENT-PHOBIC WOMAN, the appeal of an unavailable man is nearly impossible to resist. Male versions of Homer's sirens, these Levi's-clad demigods offer us the heady possibility of pleasure without a price tag, of a complicated emotional life without any of the responsibility or follow-through actual commitment tends to demand. Female commitment-phobes are tricky: Love is our Holy Grail, and we're as indomitable as Galahad in our quest for it. Only when one takes a closer look at the people we choose to pursue—men who are married or gay or who, as citizens of other countries, are accessible to us only when we break down and purchase expensive round-trip airline tickets—does our true desire become stunningly clear: We want romantic titillation, but without any of the messy rigors of genuine intimate engagement.

In the years before life became complicated with such words as *deconstructionism* and *Wonderbra*, there was a word for a woman who demonstrated the unfortunate tendency to fall for unavailable men. That word was *mistress*. Eternally damned to holidays spent in miserable, gin-soaked isolation, these women, while not exactly lacking for male companionship, when attempting to explain their sad predicament tended to rely on the justification that all the really good men were already taken. What these women may have been less likely to consider (particularly, for example, while eating old ice cream from its gummy carton and watching reruns of *Good Times* on New Year's Eve) was that the appeal of the men to whom they were habitually drawn lay precisely in their unavailability. Yes, it's a nightmare to spend every weekend alone, but perhaps less of a nightmare—assuming one is deeply terrified of intimate involvement—than attempting to negotiate contact with another person in the absence of a built-in escape narrative.

Indeed, when one's man is compelled to leap from bed at ten-thirty and race home to his center-hall Colonial, one never has to face the dreary reality of, say, conversational repetition or his attempts at compromising your decorating scheme. Furthermore, the experienced mistress rarely has to deal with the unpleasantness of revealing her vulnerable inner self to her partner, thus risking either the pain of rejection or the potential loss of her privacy. Women caught in this cycle likely believed themselves when they insisted that they longed for domestic ritual and constancy, but their actions bore out the fact that what they actually were attracted to was the excitement of superficial role playing and the safety of regular intervals of solitude.

These days, one needn't don the glamorous and stigmatized hat of the mistress in order to successfully bypass commitment. Indeed, we now have at our disposal all manner of newer, more creative methods of intimacy avoidance. Whereas once we would have been relegated to disgracing ourselves at dinner parties with other women's husbands, the options for sidestepping relationships have virtually exploded, what with every other man racing out of the closet or brunching with their inner children or hauling their bongo drums into the woods for a Robert Bly weekend retreat. Falling in love with a career bachelor works very nicely as a path to guaranteed singleness, as does an infatuation with a man who would be happier meeting your brother. If you're spending more money on your phone bill than on rent, chances are you've surrendered to the allure of the long-distance relationship, another form of faux engagement that I've sampled with considerable delectation. The bottom line is this: When the fact that you can't get a given man makes him that much more attractive, the alarm bells should already be sounding loud and clear.

Alarms are ringing around my old friend Paula, but she can't hear them. She is getting desperate. She recently celebrated her twenty-ninth birthday, and she's still emphatically single. Now, Paula is in all ways but one a completely lucid and intelligent person. After toiling to maintain her 4.0 average at a ridiculously competitive Ivy League college, she was accepted to a prestigious medical school. She endured with uncommon grace and savvy the challenges of male-dominated study sessions and cadaver dissection, and after graduating landed a lucrative if slavish internship in a huge, frenzied urban teaching hospital. She's spent the last eight months assigned to emergency room duty, which, as those of us who keep up with the network hospital dramas know, means that a typical workday can last up to forty-eight hours and tends to involve saving literally dozens of lives.

In addition to these courageous acts of medical valor, Paula manages to handle the quotidian admirably. For her, getting ready for an evening out does not mean running a dampened sponge over her food-encrusted jacket and hoping for dim lighting; instead, Paula trots her soiled garments down to the dry cleaner. She also vacuums her apartment on a regular basis and on Sunday evenings watches a moderate amount of television. She's a regular poster child for the virtues of levelheaded practicality.

Except when it comes to men. Paula is simply unable to make a reasonable assessment of a single man: The more wildly inappropriate he is, the harder she falls for him. While in conversations about my love life or those of our mutual friends, she is capable of making thoughtful observations and even issuing warnings about particularly unsavory characters, but when these same men wander into her area of vision, she is rendered sightless.

The more unlikely the match, the more passionately Paula embraces it. When she becomes interested in a man, this unflappable physician develops a childlike guilelessness, a naïveté so powerful it would require bumping into her beloved holding up a 7-Eleven in full ski-masked regalia to persuade her that he might not be the man of her dreams. Shortly after she becomes involved with one of these men, the clues begin to surface—unfamiliar articles of female clothing appearing in his bedroom, a stray earring embedded in the couch cushion, even money missing from her wallet on one occasion. Even more striking than the signs of malfeasance is her ability to ignore or rationalize them as they crop up, one after the next, creating a collective road map to disaster.

Currently, she's obsessed with an aspiring actor, Ryan, who supports himself tending bar. A dubious combination, at best, what with all the nubile young things piling into his place of employment every evening to sip Chardonnay and make eye contact with him. Ryan's not the most reliable suitor; he breaks down and calls Paula once every few weeks, just about the time she's accepted the fact that she'll never hear from him again. They get together—it's wonderful, it's heaven—and when he leaves the next morning she's exultant. But soon enough the tension sets in, and within forty-eight hours she's again anxiously eyeing the telephone, filled with anticipatory dread. This could go on for years.

Meanwhile, a fellow intern, Alan, a very nice guy who happens also to be attractive, is plainly interested in Paula. He asks her to lunch, offers advice on her more perplexing medical cases, listens to what she has to say. "He's very sweet," she admits. Then she shudders. "It kind of gives me the creeps." When I ask her to explain this, she hesitates for a moment, then says, "Somehow, he doesn't seem very masculine to me. He just doesn't have that edge." Paula is convinced that her attraction to less-than-accountable men is an unlucky accident; she believes that if she's patient enough and clever enough, the bartender will realize she's the soul mate he's been waiting for. Of course, he's waiting for no such thing—that's pretty clear—but just try telling Paula. And while there's no guarantee that a relationship with Alan would prove successful, the fact that her coworker's attentiveness and constancy turn her off makes me inclined to chalk her behavior up to a fear of getting genuinely involved with a man, rather than simply to bad taste.

If Paula were interested in having a casual relationship, if she wouldn't get weepy opening the Styles section of the *New York Times* and studying the photos of new brides, all would be copacetic. But the fact is she spends the vast majority of what little free time she has standing in her apartment, wringing her hands, and wondering if it's worth a call to AT&T to find out if the phone lines are down. Relying on the same single-minded determination that guided her through some of the most demanding academic programs to which one can gain entrance, Paula is fixated on her ability to break down Ryan's resistance and make him see fidelity's glorious light.

For a long time I didn't have a clue as to why such an apparently functional person as Paula would be possessed of such a monomaniacal need to sabotage her love prospects. How could a person who spent her day stitching up victims of subway knife fights, her shift completed and the white doctor's coat exchanged for a cocktail dress, be so thoroughly cowed by the prospect of romantic fulfillment?

Then I met her mother. Paula had over the years made the occasional comment regarding her mother's "demanding" or "hard-to-please" nature, but it wasn't until I found myself seated beside the woman at a dinner party that I began to comprehend Paula's mastery of understatement. Thin as a string and suited up in a

"Jackie goes to Dallas" suit, Paula's mother wasted no time getting to the heart of her favorite topic: Paula's career folly. Unlike most of our parents, Paula's mother takes no pleasure in the fact that her daughter spends her days and nights engaged in the saving of human lives—not while Paula's ring finger remains tragically naked. This Westchester, New York, matron is a virtual Newt Gingrich in drag, and she makes no bones about the fact that, in her opinion, the female pursuit of a professional life is beyond bad taste. In her mother's mind, Paula may as well make her living as a sex worker, so effectively has she undermined her chances for nuptial victory.

Somewhere between salad and cheese, one of the other guests at the party demonstrated the bad judgment to compliment Paula on her emergency delivery of twins earlier in the day—a day she had concluded, needless to say, by serving a sumptuous and perfectly prepared dinner to eight guests. Paula's mother sighed loudly and tossed her napkin on the table, disappearing into the bathroom for a good long visit while a paler Paula anxiously kept her gaze fixed on the closed door.

Paula's mother's exaggerated reaction to the reminder of her daughter's occupation did not exactly shock the female guests at this gathering. Who among us has not wondered with considerable trepidation whether our future happiness is contingent upon choosing between a personal and professional life? Writers from Charlotte Brontë to Virginia Woolf to Judith Krantz have spent innumerable chapters pondering this very dilemma: At what cost to a woman's private life is her work outside the home, and vice versa? And while we females born in the latter half of the century make a great show of acting as though this were a moot point ("Of course we can have it all!"), the tiny voice of our mothers or grandmothers or even the women in business suits whom we see hurling produce and baby food and vials of Excedrin into shopping carts at eight P.M. suggests that our fantasy of easily combining work and family might in fact be just that—a fantasy.

Paula is forestalling what she fears is the inevitable: Marriage will mean a surrender of the professional work that has come to mean so much to her. Her woebegone attention to the latest issue of *Sophisticated Bride* and the pages of doodles combining her first and Ryan's last name suggest that she hasn't the slightest inkling that her attraction to this perpetually elusive beau is part of a grand, and unacknowledged, plan to postpone this unpleasant decision. Because, while on an intellectual level, Paula flatly rejects her mother's version of a legitimate lifestyle, with its membership in the Junior League and days spent carpooling activity-exhausted children, emotionally Paula has bought her mother's story without a hitch. Underneath her bravado, Paula believes that any man worth his salt would, as soon as laying eyes on and claim to her, demand that she renounce her career in medicine and get down to the real work of housewifery. The anxiety she feels as her thirtieth year approaches might be irrational, but it's fairly understandable, given that her mother's birthday gift will most likely be a prescription for hormone replacement drugs.

Paula has allowed herself one enormous act of rebellion: becoming a doctor. Unfortunately, the barbaric guilt she feels at having done so has effectively prevented her from closely examining the outdated expectations her family has heaped upon her. And it's an examination she will have to make, for until she does she'll be unable to decide which of her family's values she can accept and which don't fit. Until Paula rejects the notion that she's digging her own marital grave by pursuing work she enjoys, she'll continue to gravitate toward men who have no more serious or long-term interest in her than Ryan does. That, or she'll give in and abandon medicine, passing her days instead contemplating chintz window treatments and her increasing fondness for Valium.

And then there's Annie. We all know or have met someone like her. Sophisticated and urbane, she is the sort of thirtysomething citified woman who has taken the art of aesthetic discernment to a new and (to we of the less-hip swinish multitudes) savagely intimidating level. Having spent so much time and energy cultivating her particular edgy sensibility, she's ascended to that rarefied level of chic that manages to exclude pretty much everybody at the party. Though naturally quite attractive, Annie has turned her appearance into a kind of statement, dyeing her dark brown hair platinum and never leaving the house without lipstick so red it looks black. With her ultrapale, UV-deprived skin, to the uninitiated she might easily be mistaken for an extra in a vampire film rather than the midwestern girl she actually is.

Though I'd heard about Annie for many years from mutual friends, I didn't get the chance to meet her until those friends, having decided to marry, enlisted Annie to take their wedding photos. A professional photographer by trade—one who typically spends her days snapping A-list celebrity models for slick, overscented magazines—Annie made no secret of the fact that she was mortified by this low-rent task. To her, such work was the equivalent of Kate Moss condescending to pose for a JCPenney catalog.

Annie's distress on this particular day was compounded by her conviction that she herself would never don a bridal costume. "This is about as close as I'll ever get to wedded bliss," she muttered as I passed her a glass of champagne. She nodded toward our friend, the bride. "Maybe if I'm nice, she'll let me wear her veil." As Annie continued to click away, I couldn't help but notice that her date for the evening, a stunningly handsome Brad Pitt look-alike, was making not-terribly-covert moon eyes at the groom.

Now, I adore gay men. Given the choice of spending time with a man who'll discuss his—or your—feelings until both your teeth ache versus one who rolls his eyes when you mention your current water-weight bloat, it's a decision that really makes itself. Consequently, I spend as much time with gay men as a person humanly can, and I am vastly the better for it. But I came to a decision many years ago that has also served me well, and it is this:

Gay men are not for dating. Not for going to bed with and not for falling in love with, difficult to avoid though the latter might sometimes be. Women are forever going back on this resolve—understandable when you think of how pleasant the company of such men is, and the ease with which the both of you seem to understand each other. But when a woman makes such assignations a habit, there's trouble brewing.

Obviously, certain professions attract a more creative, unconventional sort of man, and given the nature of Annie's job—fashion photography—it's hardly surprising that she has developed a die-hard addiction to men who, through no fault of hers or theirs, are not in a position to offer the kind of romantic commitment for which she yearns. During the period when we were first getting to know each other, Annie was immersed in a string of fantasy liaisons with a cadre of charming and *mignon* gentlemen whose unifying feature was that, romantically, they didn't know Annie was alive. During this time she seemed fairly content to attribute her dubious romantic choices to simple heterosexual scarceness. The fact that a large percentage of the men she met at work (models, set or clothing designers, stylists) were, by nature of their sexual preference, inappropriate love matches for her was sufficient explanation for the dead-end crushes she was constantly developing.

But as time passed and we got to know one another better, I began to think that there might be more to Annie's consistencies of taste than the "industry" explanation she routinely relied on. I decided to pursue this line of inquiry while we were having dinner at a shadowy Soho bistro that was at that time one of her favorite haunts. And why not? Black-clad artists and models and waitpersons milled around the place, indistinguishable from one another. Annie had been surreptitiously eyeing the bartender, a dead ringer for a young Rock Hudson, when I leaned toward her and whispered, "What's going on with you? This place is full of straight men, all your exact type, and you're checking out the bartender."

"But he's adorable!" she protested.

"That's because he's wearing mascara," I said snippily. "What have you got against heterosexuals?"

"I'm terrified of them," she answered in her usual blunt manner. "I'm not kidding. The less likely a guy is to want me, the more I like him." She started to laugh as she confessed, "I don't know what I'd do with a straight man. Other than drive him crazy."

Obsessed though she was by the procurement of romantic happiness, Annie was equally frightened of true connection with a man. She warded off her specific demons in a couple of ways. First, while she recognized on some level that the guys at work were probably not going to revise their own profoundly incompatible sexual inclinations to match hers, she continued to engage in a strenuous, if absolutely unreciprocal, romantic discourse with them. She was remarkably stubborn about misreading signals, so that a friendly invitation for a drink after working hours would send her flying to the ladies' room to apply yet another layer of blood-red lipstick and regel her short-cropped hair. And when the friendly drink remained exactly that—no furtively bumping knees, no good-night kiss—she would return forlornly to her apartment, utterly dejected.

In addition to her penchant for fantasy, Annie also put her overly critical sensibility to use in avoiding fruitful interactions with straight men. Because she is in fact a very warm and loving person whose self-protective instincts are wildly out of control, it's hard to watch her routinely sabotaging encounters with those straight men who do demonstrate interest in her. Any cultural event, whether it's a play or movie or photo shoot, is subject to her intense and sometimes arbitrary (though not to her) critical eye, and woe to the straight man who disagrees with her divine pronouncement. And, worse, she trains this eagle eye on the men themselves, so that the most minute percentage of synthetic in a dress shirt or a southwestern-influenced belt buckle can turn an otherwise respectable suitor into a modern-day Quasimodo.

Annie describes her childhood as freakish. "Unfortunately, I was the freak." She grew up on a ranch in Idaho, where her parents and all manner of ranch hands raised large quantities of odoriferous cattle. She claims she can remember lying in her crib and thinking, "Where the hell am I?" a sentiment that, even assuming a certain amount of poetic license, conveys her general sense of alienation from her surroundings.

In any event, and unlike her two female siblings, Annie did not exhibit the pink good looks and milk-fed roundness so applauded in farm children. Those of us more broad of beam have to suspend our disbelief a mite to sympathize with the hardship of growing up wafer thin and willowy, but as they say in real estate, location is everything. On more than one occasion her rural farmer father, in response to his daughter's balking at another carbohydrate-heavy meal, threatened to string her up in the vegetable garden and put her to work as a scarecrow. And more than once, on her family's rare excursions into town, she had the discomfiting experience of being mistaken for a boy, something that did not help to subvert her fear that her femininity was somehow flawed, insufficient.

As time passed, Annie's older sisters began to partake of the usual high school crushes and backseat make-out festivals, a development that, in spite of Annie's feigned indifference, contributed further to her sorry feelings of isolation. Because her specific physical appeal did not correspond to the narrow definition of beauty in that small, remote town, she regrettably concluded that her particular attributes would not translate anywhere. Thus she set upon her years-long avoidance of the romantic universe, a world she believed could offer her only abject and unspeakable rejection.

Annie had always been intensely interested in art, deriving enormous pleasure from sketching or painting the dramatic landscape around her. And though her artistic development offered her much badly needed direction and satisfaction, it also served to further distance her from the ruminatively hay-chewing people who were enlisted with raising her. By the time she discovered photography, her poor parents had essentially abandoned their hope that she would come to her senses and get interested in cattle. It seems not an accident that such an experienced outsider as Annie would choose photography as her profession, as it is a practice whose salient feature is its neat removal of the practitioner from the center of activity. She was eminently more comfortable depicting a thing's surface than she was taking the risk of reaching beyond and into its core.

Even once she escaped Idaho and began to establish herself as a photographer in New York, and despite the rather substantial professional success she soon began to enjoy, Annie privately and fervently sustained the conviction of her own personal inadequacy. Over the years, she's had a few brief relationships, but at a certain point in the developing closeness, she always hits a snag—misinterpreting a neutral comment as critical, or concluding suddenly that the man she was crazy about only weeks ago is, in fact, "a total loser." After the dust from these romantic misfires settles, and she is returned to her clear-headed state, she gradually comes to recognize that she has been controlling events with her own strong inclination to bolt once the possibility of true emotional closeness surfaces. At this point, despite her persistent doubts that any man will find her genuinely and lastingly attractive, Annie is determined to break this pattern of staggering blindly away from intimacy as if it were a wrecked car whose gas tank was about to explode.

Not long ago, at Annie's insistence, we attended a benefit for a local politician about whom she was keen (I remembered to slip a Sony Watchman into my overstuffed pocketbook, just in case things got dull), and while we were sipping our mauve-colored cocktails, a nice-looking man approached. Obedient practitioner of social intercourse, I automatically smiled, but when I glanced over at Annie, I saw that her pleasant face was pinched into something resembling a grimace. The man chatted with us for a few minutes, until my abject ignorance of local government became impossible to ignore, whereupon he turned his attention to Annie. Wowed by her whiplike grasp of referendums and the like, this gentleman concluded the conversation by requesting her phone number. Reluctantly, she handed it over.

After he'd moved out of earshot I gave the usual gleeful scream signaling a social touchdown, to which Annie responded sternly, "Shut up!" When I asked what was wrong—what could be wrong, given that the gods had just smiled upon us?—she hissed, "Oh, why did I do that? Now I'm going to have to have my number changed." When I appeared dumbfounded, she added, "He's obviously a serial killer. Didn't you see those eyes?" Well, friends, I had, but apparently those twinkling pools of cerulean, Aidan Quinn blue had had a very different effect on Annie than on me. And while I'm all for going with one's instincts and avoiding homicidal maniacs, it was clear that, in her judgment of this perfectly pleasant fellow, she was deranged.

But she's trying. For one thing, at the scolding insistence of me and all our other friends, Annie decided to retain her telephone number. And when her prospective beau made good on his promise to call, she even consented to go on a date with him. They've seen each other a few times, and while she is excruciatingly tentative as each new stage of potential intimacy approaches—agreeing to allow her new friend to pick her up at her actual apartment on their third date, for instance, sent her into a frenzied tailspin of anxiety—she's determined to at least attempt to suspend her disbelief regarding the very real likelihood of his sincere interest.

Annie has begun to see that one way to let go of the hideous assumptions about her own unworthiness that have so dominated her interactions with men is to allow herself to have experiences that challenge her insecurities. If she manages to welcome the attention of an interested man, rather than respond with her typical arrogance or arch impatience, she will begin the process of subverting those negative assumptions that have functioned mainly to reinforce the isolation she hates. Instead of protecting her from pain, Annie's force field of sophisticated nervosity has trapped her in a kind of luxury prison from which she is finally, happily, beginning to escape. So far, she's only requested weekend passes, but soon, one hopes, she'll apply for parole.

It's the rare and vigilant woman who hasn't at one time or another fallen under the spell of long-distance romance. The delights of faraway love are almost too numerous to list, though the most undeniably compelling benefit is the chance such liaisons offer of turning ordinary romantic interaction into something magical, something outside of normative experience — love on an extended vacation during which one's luggage never gets lost.

When you begin a relationship with someone who lives in another city or (even better) country, you enter a beautifully controlled universe over which you have been, somewhat remarkably, granted absolute rule. The fact that this universe — so persuasive are its pleasures — bears not even a passing resemblance to real life can be ignored almost indefinitely. When you have to board a train to commune with Eros, you have the option of presenting whomever you wish to your inamarato, regardless of how similar or dissimilar your holiday self might be to the real you. Left at the platform is the person who weeps during encore presentations of the Hallmark Hall of Fame or explodes in a rage when her dry cleaning is not ready. And if the wondrous fantasy self sashaying through romantic weekends with your distant beau is a far cry from the you who spends entire days sitting on the couch and whimpering, you can bet that the person courting you over all those miles is none too similar to the warty self he hauls into work every morning. Strangers on and off the train are what you and your paramour are, and so you will remain for as long as your relationship is located in the never-never land of Amtrak or Delta.

Jesus Wept

When it comes to love at a distance, Sarah is widely regarded as the local expert, holding perhaps the world record for dating guys outside her area code. She spent the better part of her twenties trying to dodge phone company credit departments and abusing the WATTS line at her place of employment simply in order to maintain communication with her string of long-distance loves. When her birthday or Christmas rolled around, friends knew in advance the perfect and absolutely necessary gift: cash. Sarah was trying to sustain her own brand of addiction, one that required not hypodermic needles or jars of sour mash, but a lightweight travel iron and an updated passport.

When I met Sarah, she was at the height, though sadly not the conclusion, of her obsession with frequent-flier mileage. She was involved with Tim, a man she'd met in college. Too "shy" to start something up with him while they shared the same dormitory bathroom, she waited until Tim had accepted a position teaching English to Chinese students and was days away from boarding a plane to Beijing before divulging her romantic feelings for him. Sarah and her new beloved spent the three days preceding his journey in bed, making ardent pronouncements and drinking inexpensive Chilean wine.

For those of you who've never tried it, sustaining a relationship with a resident of Asia isn't exactly the most stress-free of endeavors. In addition to the radical difference in time zones, there's the fact of greatly delayed mail service, outrageously priced telephone communication, and long periods between visits. And yet Sarah persevered, forcing herself to learn the phrases required to negotiate with impatient Chinese telephone operators. Although she had never experienced any desire to see China, let alone move there, she began contemplating doing exactly that, in spite of the fact that she'd recently landed a fantasy job in magazine publishing, one that couldn't be replicated in Beijing.

Because Sarah and her beau had become involved just as he was changing countries, they were forced to undertake the business of getting to know each other from half a planet away. She was thus vulnerable to what we experts know as the "obsessed with a virtual stranger" phenomenon. When letters and phone calls are the only means of communing with one's beloved, it's remarkably easy to see what you want to and ignore anything you don't. Attempting to delve into another's soul, to ascertain his values or even successfully divine what he ate for dinner, isn't easy when battling transpacific phone-line delay, but Sarah did her best. Despite her efforts, however, by the time Tim arrived home for his weeklong stay, she had developed a picture of him that was, succinctly speaking, incomplete.

Sarah's correspondence with Tim had been decidedly high-toned—discussing the finer points of Rilke or arguing about which film, *The Seventh Seal* or *Ran*, would enjoy a more enduring place in the history of cinema—so she felt confident about the shape that their visit would take, and planned accordingly. She imagined the two of them wandering through the Museum of Modern Art, Cha-galls and Picassos gazing benevolently upon them, or indulging in an overpriced and romantic French meal at one of the many fancy restaurants whose facades she had wistfully passed on her way to and from the office. So it came as a surprise when she awakened after their first night together—a night during which Tim had evi-denced very little interest in touching her—to find him standing in her darkened kitchen, drinking room-temperature vodka straight out of the bottle.

"What did you do?" I asked her, aghast at her description of this scene.

"I said, 'Excuse me,' and flipped off the light. Then I sat down in the living room and started chewing on my hand."

Tim spent most of the following five days in a state of such extreme intoxication that Sarah was compelled to wake herself each night to make sure he was still breathing. They did very little talking during Tim's stay, their conversation limited to the profoundly work-manlike: "Is there any more beer?" or "What time do the liquor stores close?" Alternately shocked and angry, Sarah spent the week in dumbfounded silence, knowing only that there was nothing she could do to salvage the situation.

Once Tim had gathered his things and departed, Sarah was left on her own to clear away the empties and recover. She slowly began to assess the events of the last several months, rereading Tim's letters, this time not in the state of anticipatory elation but instead with the cool and objective eye of the recently burned. She saw that between explications of the lesser-known works of Byron and Shelley, Tim had interspersed all manner of hints about his romantic ambivalence, including lengthy descriptions about the carousingly wild time he was having abroad and the various ways in which he was enjoying his self-imposed exile. In retrospect, especially the retrospect of his horrifying behavior, Tim's unease regarding their union seemed almost laughably obvious. But Sarah, in her single-minded determination to see things in a way that suited her purposes, had been utterly blind to it.

Sarah was brought pretty low by her experience with Tim, not only because their time together had been such an unmitigated nightmare, but also because she'd lost the consuming focus that had occupied her time so nicely. When, after a few weeks of watching hair-care infomercials until three A.M., her colleague Louisa invited her to a small dinner get-together, Sarah made up her mind to attend.

As it happened, Louisa, who was originally from Scotland, was entertaining a cousin, Ben, from her hometown of Glasgow. With his cheerful accent and his warm manner, Ben seemed almost too good to be true—the perfect antidote to the alcoholic-houseguest blues. In addition to his disposition, he had to his credit a strapping, farming-in-the-blood, broad-shouldered frame and those rosy British cheeks that suggest either wildly good health or an early consumptive death. Sarah chose to attribute Ben's complexion to the former and prepared herself to be charmed. Dinner was a grand, drunken success, which concluded with Ben's escorting Sarah to a cab and bestowing upon her a knee-weakening good-night kiss.

And so began a week of bliss. Ben moved his suitcases to Sarah's apartment and sweetly persuaded her to call in sick to work, a request she was happy to oblige. With Ben she was able to have the kind of magical holiday that Tim's delirium tremens had prevented, and she was enchanted by his open, curious mind, his old-world courtesy, his nocturnal vigor. Scotland started looking better and better as a place to raise children, and she threw herself wholeheartedly into mentally decorating the stone-walled, thatched-roof cottage she was certain they would one day purchase. It was Brontë country, she told herself, amazed at the good fortune awaiting her.

So it was a sad day, indeed, when Ben boarded his plane home. Fortunately, Sarah's heartache was mitigated by the elaborate plans the two had already concocted for their next visit. She continued to hoard her pennies, and happily, not two months later, she was strapping herself into a 747, swallowing four Valium, and praying that the cargo area was free of explosive devices. Ben met her at the airport and the two spent three glorious days traveling around the bucolic, impossibly green Scottish countryside.

Everything was perfect—or nearly perfect—until the time came for Ben to bring her home to meet his family. True, Sarah had noticed a few qualities in Ben that had eluded her on his visit to her city: a certain rigidity, a bit of a temper, a very pronounced intellectual defensiveness. But this did not initially concern her, who had abandoned a Ph.D. in literature to embark on her magazine career and in general considered herself to be a bit of a bully on subjects academic. So when Ben would withdraw into sullenness after an especially heated debate, she tended to think it was she who was at fault. She did not consider that his moodiness might be a function of his basic dislike of women. That is, until she met his father.

Ben's father, a man whose face had lost its war with broken capillaries, had cultivated none of his son's supposed tolerance of thinking females. Ben's father brooked no dissent from his own wife, Ben's mother, a woman who silently performed her household duties and discreetly vanished from sight. Later Sarah would learn that it was precisely this chauvinistic attitude that had driven her friend Louisa to seek refuge across an ocean, but during the time of her visit, Sarah was less than prepared for the cool reception awaiting her.

Had she to contend only with Ben's father and his repeated request that she restrict herself to speaking only when spoken to, it's possible that Sarah might have been able to glide smoothly through this meeting, secure in the knowledge of Ben's solidarity and affection. Unfortunately, her exposure to Ben's father offered her unwelcome insight into the mysterious feelings of unease she'd been having since her arrival about Ben himself. She saw that his stated appreciation of modern, intelligent women was his own brand of rebellion, and that her function in this game was solely as Ben's pawn. Worse, she saw that the rebellion was empty: Ben was a carbon copy of his father, and it was only with the most extreme self-control, coupled with his desire to defy his father, that he himself resisted the urge to put her in her place.

Sarah was relieved when her departure date arrived, and she took the opportunity during her flight home to gulp complimentary glasses of wine and reflect on her soured visit. And though she was disappointed, she was also forced to admit that her "surprise" about Ben was slightly disingenuous. She recalled certain conversations during which she had expressed an assertive opinion and been met with silence—something she had mistaken for circumspection or, worse, admiration, only to have the phone call quickly come to an end. She remembered reading his letters and being surprised by his markedly parochial attitudes; surprised, but also confident that her more worldly perspective would necessarily and effortlessly broaden his. She saw that, instead of falling in love with the reality of who Ben was, she had concentrated her affection on those things about him that she believed she could change. It occurred to Sarah that she might not be the only one feeling misunderstood and betrayed.

Duly chastened, Sarah stepped onto American soil filled with the resolve to steer clear of long-distance involvements. There was too much margin for error, she concluded, too much room for her fantasies to flourish unchecked. She was so determined to keep this vow that when, at a housewarming party given by some friends, she was introduced to an interesting-looking man—"Sarah! Come meet Tony. He's from Boston!"—she steadfastly ignored the palpable attraction between them. Though she enjoyed talking with him, appreciated his solicitous sense of humor and his thoughtful replenishing of her drink, she remained determined to keep their contact casual and friendly.

When she returned home from work a few days later and noticed the ominous red blink of her answering machine, Sarah hesitated before pressing the play button. And sure enough, when she finally relented, her tape spewed forth a message from Tony: "Turns out I'll be in New York again next weekend. Is there any chance we could get together?" Tempted though she was to erase and forget the communiqué, Sarah lyingly persuaded herself it would be unacceptably impolite to do so. She lifted her telephone receiver and within minutes had committed to a weekend date.

When Sarah's friends expressed their surprise, even their exasperation, that she was contemplating yet another long-distance courtship, she laughed and told them, "At least he's in the same time zone." Because being involved with a man seemed such an incredibly important goal to her, these friends persisted, wondering why she would choose to live in a state of almost constant deprivation, always either longing to see or recovering from a visit from her current beau. Wouldn't she be happier with a man who could, say, stop by after work for an evening of television or meet her for a quick sandwich during her lunch hour? One she didn't have to dial eleven or more numbers in order to reach by telephone? Sarah's explanation ("But these are the only guys I meet! It's not my fault!") left these friends unsatisfied, especially as she remained unwilling to consider that her passionate devotion to her distant-lover-of-the-moment might make it difficult for any of the men who resided more locally to approach her.

The blueprint for Sarah's relationships is likely painfully clear by now, and I needn't bore you with the particulars of her affair with Tony ("He's from Boston!"). Sarah became instantly infatuated, spent several months more or less drunk with love, and, after it became clear that Tony was not precisely the person she imagined him to be, she was once again utterly devastated. It was after this third strike that she was finally forced to examine her own motivations for taking on relationships against which the odds were so stacked from the onset.

I know this because I ran into her at a party and, while we were catching up, I couldn't help but notice the compulsive manner in which she asked every man who approached us where he was currently living. Anyone who was not a resident of our city was rapidly dispatched. Finally, left alone for a moment, I asked Sarah if she was changing her romantic standards, vis-à-vis geography and, ruefully, she admitted she was. I pressed on, wondering aloud, between generous mouthfuls of Doritos, what it was about her long-distance arrangements that had been so attractive to her.

"I guess it's the control I like," she admitted, making sure no one around us was eavesdropping. "I don't mean controlling what other people do, necessarily. More that you can reveal exactly what you want about yourself when your contact with a person is so limited. Anything I didn't like about myself just disappeared when I was with one of these guys. Assuming that I didn't slip."

Now that she'd started, there was no stopping her. It was apparent that Sarah had given her situation serious thought. "And even though it is sometimes hard to deal with the time apart, you have to consider the alternatives. I mean, the truth is that in a regular relationship your time with the person can become so boring and mundane. You bicker about things like who's hiding the television remote or not doing the laundry. If you see a guy once or twice a month, you get to sidestep all that petty bullshit. The time you spend together is perfect, because it has to be. You make it so."

When I asked her whether that didn't add a lot of pressure to these at-a-distance couplings, Sarah sighed. "Of course it does. Any tiny argument blows way out of proportion, especially if you haven't resolved it by the time you have to leave. But the pressure's not the worst of it.

"The really dangerous thing about getting involved with a guy who lives elsewhere is the tricks your mind can play. Not only do you reveal only a part of yourself, which already makes the relationship feel sort of inauthentic, but you also have the luxury, or the curse, of seeing whatever you want to in your boyfriend. You can convince yourself he's whatever you want him to be, and it really doesn't matter if you're deluded. It didn't to me, anyway. Not, at least, until I was forced to face the real person."

Sarah has decided to take a little time off from relationships, to figure out exactly what's behind her aversion to physical accessibility in a mate. She'll need to gain some insight into her fears before she can begin to conquer them, thereby making possible more geographically friendly courtship. Although during this period of relative hibernation, she feels slightly nervous about ending up like Miss Havisham, it seems clear that her steadily increasing self-knowledge will save Sarah from a future of disintegrating wedding dresses and lunatic isolation.

Objectifying one's partner—bestowing such extreme importance upon a single characteristic that it eclipses all others—has
traditionally been viewed as an exclusively masculine practice. Consequently, we tend to think of objectification as something that men
do to women, particularly women with firm and bountiful breasts.
But the ability to limit our view of a partner, focusing only on those
aspects of him or her that serve our private (and often unacknowledged) purposes, is a game at which many women have also proven
wildly successful.

When a woman is repeatedly drawn to men with whom genuine closeness is impossible—because they are married or gay or
living in Iceland—the chances are good that she is getting exactly
what she wants. When the failure of a given relationship is essentially
guaranteed, we never have to worry about making good on our
romantic promises, or sustaining our long-term feelings for another
person, or even being seen naked from behind. We can fling ourselves wholeheartedly into love without any fear, because the entire
experience is spurious and, ultimately, we know it. If you ever hear
yourself plaintively demanding, "Am I wrong for trying to hold on
to the best thing I ever had?" the answer is almost certainly a
resounding yes.

There's nothing wrong with going through the romantic dress-
rehearsals that are these dalliances with unavailable men, as long as
we're willing to admit to ourselves what we're doing. Those of us
who aren't so willing, who remain blithely mystified as we lament
our damnable romantic judgment, run the risk of developing a
dangerous taste for unrequited love. As those of us who have been
there know, unrequited love, while it may seem to be a heroic
refusal to let love die in spite of rationality and horrendous odds,
bears very little relationship to the real thing. Falling in love with
someone whom you can't possibly know or who you know can't
return your feelings is about the desire for protection, as much

as sealing oneself off in a tomb might be. But just as with refuge in a sarcophagus, while loving the unavailable may briefly make you feel safe, ultimately it will leave you trapped and gasping rather miserably for air. Not to mention the havoc it will wreak on your complexion.

6

Ordinary People Moments

Commitment Phobia
and Control

O VER THE PAST FEW YEARS we've witnessed a proliferation of movies (*Final Analysis, Mr. Jones*, and, of course, the inimitable *Prince of Tides*) whose common premise seems to be that patients seek psychological counseling not for enlightenment or restored mental health, but in order to be taken to bed. So ubiquitous is this cinematic trend that one is left wondering whether it doesn't represent a kind of revenge-driven backlash against the therapeutic community from all the outraged film executives whose penchant for dating prepubescents has been challenged during their personal fifty-minute hours.

Amusing though these recent films have been, I prefer to harken back to the golden age of shrink movies: the seventies. Those were good days, what with Jill Clayburgh's character finding herself in *An Unmarried Woman* and Peter Firth's character tragically failing on a similar quest in *Equus*. And of course, there's the seminal work, the sine qua non of therapy films, *Ordinary People*. As all of us who sat through it rapt and weeping know, this movie presents Judd Hirsch as the kindly if gruff therapist who helps darling high school student Conrad (Timothy Hutton) come to terms with his brother's accidental drowning. Conrad, who is ridden with guilt, maintains that he is angry with himself for his failure, during a boating accident, to save his brother's life. In a series of balletic moves, Hirsch's character manages to reveal to Conrad that the boy is furious not with himself but with his hulk of a brother for letting go of the boat and sinking to his death. Conrad's true feelings seem to him unspeakably disloyal, so much so that he would rather off himself than betray his brother by admitting to them. And yet when he finally does acknowledge his anger, what Conrad actually feels is tremendous, glorious relief.

If you've spent any time at all on a therapist's couch (or even watched an episode or two of *Ricki Lake*), chances are you're familiar with the concept of overcompensation. It's not complicated: When you think your response to a given situation is somehow flawed, you try to conceal it by doing the opposite. A fairly commonplace example is the die-hard cheapskate who makes a huge show of buying the first round of drinks in a bar. His friends hoist their frosty, delicious beverages, delighted that their companion is such a generous fellow; meanwhile, said fellow is awash with the glory of knowing his wallet will not have to make another appearance for the duration of the evening.

Because Mr. Cheapskate is so secretly terrified that he's a miser, he needs to resort to large public displays indicating the opposite. Perversely, however, his gestures do not persuade him that he's transcended his penny-pinching ways. Quite the opposite, in fact; for inherent in the very magnaminity of the gesture is the confirmation of his worst fears—he's so horribly stingy that he has to hide behind a big show of false beneficence. The most confounding aspect of this arrangement is that, as in Conrad's case, the truth that the overcompensator wishes to conceal is generally far more innocuous than the behavior undertaken to disguise it.

Not surprisingly, the overcompensatory fictions employed by the women in this chapter tend to keep them relatively safe from romantic intimacy. These women are like little fiends working to persuade not only their potential dream dates but also themselves that they really are the people they present, regardless of how true or false these presentations are. As a result, they stay strangers to their partners for as long as possible, much as they are determined to remain strangers to themselves. And when everybody's a stranger, intimacy simply doesn't happen, no matter how often said strangers wake up in each other's beds.

While speaking with each of the women in this chapter, I had a flash of what I think of as an Ordinary People Moment, when I suddenly saw the narrative each was offering as the exact opposite of the emotional truth of their situations. These women aren't exactly liars; they're simply trying really, really hard to convince themselves. They're slippery and, given this, it's our job as disciples of Mr. Hirsch's venerable psychologist to act as detectives, to reach beyond the surface these women are working so hard to maintain and get at the real story.

I met Eva a few years ago at a party. I had noticed her when she arrived, for she was someone to whom my mother would have paid her highest compliment: Eva was "put together." Tall and shapely, she wore her cool blond hair swept up in some kind of no doubt difficult-to-achieve but simple-looking French twist and was dressed from head to toe in black crepe. Of course, as the occasion for the party was a gallery opening in Soho, everyone present looked as though they were attending a very chic funeral.

Like me, Eva makes her own hours, but unlike me she doesn't waste them studying the celebrity gossip columns in *Vanity Fair*. She is employed by one of the city's august museums, performing the ancient and painstaking job of art restoration, which as far as I can gather is a kind of paint-by-numbers touch-up of the Old Masters. By all reports she is a tremendously gifted artwork mender, though how she can sit for long hours amid all those nauseating chemical smells is beyond me. Eva speaks vaguely about the time when she'll concentrate on her own painting, but this is a sketchy and somewhat desultory plan. For the time being, she seems content to restore order to the universe of art history.

Eva is an exceptionally composed person, easygoing to an extreme, possessed of an apparently impenetrable serenity. Though cheerful and intelligent, she seems emotionally unflappable, coping with such typical daily upsets as the washing machine's overflow or the receipt of one's American Express bill with amused good humor. This placidity extends to her physical universe as well; she moves with the restrained fluidity of a Madonna (and not the one renowned for her conical undergarments and lapsed popularity). When first getting to know her, I mistook Eva's geniality for a kind of flower-child spaciness, a nouveau-hippie beatification, but that impression didn't last long. Beneath her apparent repose beats a careful, controlled heart. She's not unlike someone paused in the eye of a storm, ever watchful of its impending progress.

As a teenager, Eva had been the kind of girl that boys pursued. By the time she was fifteen, boys were calling her up on the telephone and asking her out on dates, during which they took her to places like the movies and actually paid for both tickets. To me this is fascinating information, and I have irritated Eva more times than I care to remember, forcing her to regale me with stories of coed camping trips and an escort on prom night. (This is probably because I spent the evening of my dateless junior prom rereading *The Bell Jar*, consumed with jealousy that my best friend had been asked to attend. That is, until the next morning at five A.M. when said friend called to say that her boyfriend had broken up with her in a Dunkin' Donuts just before the dance began. She had then gone to the prom and proceeded to set fire to the tablecloth with the candle in the orange chrysanthemum centerpiece. But that's another story.)

In any event, Eva glided into this potentially flammable world of dating with very little trauma. She was interested in social life, but she was not particularly interested in falling in love. Other people's love for her was fine, so long as she could collect and not be forced to return it. This kind of power distribution was already familiar, as her own parents had thoughtfully supplied the model. In her parents' case, Eva's father had the power and her mother did not. This power inequity was partly the result of her parents' markedly different natures—her father's being critical and confrontational, her mother's, conciliatory. And it probably also had something to do with the fact that Eva's father had a salary and her mother an allowance. But we all know how that song goes. All Eva had to do was pick which role she preferred and begin emulating. She chose her father's.

Eva's pattern went as follows: She would spy some particularly delectable specimen (I always imagine that they looked like the glum yet dazzling Jordan Catalano on *My So-Called Life*) and decide that he would be the object of her obsession. She'd fantasize about him, gaze at him surreptitiously in study hall, hope that he'd be at the fall football rallies. Eventually, rumor would get around of her interest, or the guy himself would transcend that standard high school obtuseness and notice her noticing him, and then (this is the mystifying part, but I'm game) he'd start to like her back. Shortly after this development, he'd ask her out. And once this had occurred, she would instantly lose interest. She didn't really want to get to know any of these guys, and she certainly didn't want to get involved in any backseat carnal gropings. She just wanted to know that they liked her, and once it was clear that they did, off she went to the next conquest.

Back then, Eva was interested in control; she still is. To be in control, she feels, ensures that she has the power in any given situation. It would be easy to look at this desire as dangerous or mean-spirited, as the very word *power* tends to suggest the possibility of its misuse. However, if we don our Judd Hirsch psychologist caps and assume his penetrating but compassionate laser-beam gaze, it becomes evident that Eva's desire for power is not so much for the egoist thrill of acquiring it, but for what she hopes this power will give her. She wants to be safe, and her need for control—and the power it confers—suggests that she doesn't feel particularly so. Which gives us some insight into her career choice: What's more orderly than returning an already completed masterpiece to its original and completely predestined glory? It's the perfect antidote to the anxiety-inducing disorder of an empty canvas.

When Eva was in her middle twenties she became involved with a medical student named Sam. With his Clark Kent good looks and his steady, ambitious nature, Sam was everything her mother (or anybody's mother, for that matter) could have wanted. Eva worried, every now and then, that Sam was wrong for her, too conventional or staid, but he was so clearly in love with her and so plainly a good catch that she tried to ignore her doubts.

Doing so was made easier by the fact that Eva was so firmly in control of her relationship with Sam, a man possessed of a distinctly malleable nature. On the infrequent occasions when he defied her, insisting on having his way on some issue, defiance was exactly what it felt like to Eva, a child rebelling against his strict parent. One of her close friends, Susan, who works with her at the museum, would listen to Eva arguing on the telephone with Sam about plans for the evening or something he'd said the night before that had displeased her. Eva describes concluding one such conversation and hanging up the phone to find Susan staring at her. "Who," Susan asked, aghast, "were you talking to?" When Eva admitted it had been Sam, Susan shook her head. "Jesus," she exclaimed, "please, please promise you'll never speak to me like that, okay?"

Upon graduation, Sam was accepted at a prestigious hospital in Ohio for his residency. He tried to persuade Eva to move across the country with him, but she was unwilling to leave her job, especially as there were no comparable museums in the area to which Sam was relocating. Furthermore, given Sam's level of devotion, Eva was confident that the relationship would survive the yearlong separation and that he would return to her area as soon as possible. After agreeing to a fairly frequent visiting schedule, Sam left for Ohio.

So, it came as a surprise when Sam suggested that Eva delay her first visit. And she was surprised again when Sam decided to delay his own plans to visit her city. His internship, he explained, was far more intensive than he'd anticipated, and he needed to adjust to the rigorous schedule before he could relax enough to enjoy her company. This went on for months, during which time Eva found herself increasingly anxious. She grilled him about his reluctance to see her, demanding to know the real reason, but Sam insisted that the problem was his workload and nothing more. During this period she found herself thinking about Sam far more frequently than she ever had before and missing his company with a fervor that surprised her. Although she had always found temptations of the flesh difficult to resist, she found herself distinctly uninterested in soothing her loneliness with the company of another man.

When the news came—not from Sam but from a mutual friend of theirs—that her beloved not only had a new girlfriend but was in fact living with this woman, Eva felt as though she'd been tossed out of a moving vehicle. Her whole body was paralyzed with panicked dread, and she staggered around the apartment for what felt like hours. Eva remained in this sickened, horror-struck state for many weeks, through angry, accusatory phone calls with Sam, through sleepless nights. She felt like she was in hell.

"It was everything I'd tried to avoid, that feeling of being tricked, taken by surprise. Even though I knew something like this must be going on, I'd just refused to believe it. Sam was the one who wanted to get married, to have children with me. I couldn't believe how completely I'd been fooled." Eva could not be consoled by the fact that her feelings for Sam had sometimes been less than solid, that she'd often felt contempt for him or not respected his thoughts and feelings. By persuading her that he loved her, then getting involved with another woman and not even bothering to let Eva know, Sam had whisked control of the situation out of her hands.

Having her worst nightmare come true took its toll on Eva. She had spent her whole life in a strenuous avoidance of the loss of control, overcompensating by entering relationships like hers with Sam, in which her feelings were decidedly less intense than her partner's. And in spite of her efforts, she found herself in freefall, utterly taken by surprise, with no recourse. The part of herself she'd tried to suppress, the frightened Eva who believed herself utterly powerless, had surfaced with a vengeance.

Now, while it obviously wasn't Eva's fault that her Prince Charming had turned into such an unmitigated toad, the experience was nevertheless relevant. She now sees that she was interested in Sam not because he was a catch, but because she believed she could control him and thus reinforce her frantic hope that she could maintain the upper hand in their courtship. And when this hope was so cruelly dashed, and she was tossed out on her ear, she was forced to examine the apprehensions that made safety a bigger priority than emotional authenticity in her relationships.

During this period of self-reflection, Eva took a bit of a breather from dating. When she finally resumed a social life, she was careful to restrict herself to dating men about whom she could keep her feelings casual. Human nature being what it is, her cool reserve was alluring to the opposite sex and she had plenty of options for a standing date each Saturday night. But, as in the past, once one of her suitors evidenced interest in moving toward commitment, she'd begin to withdraw, compelled more by the thrill of acquisition than the reality of possession.

When she met Peter, her current boyfriend, the last thing she expected was a serious involvement. Peter was living in Boston, where he'd gotten a master's degree in public policy and was working as an advocate for that city's homeless population. Having already suffered the indignities and bitter pitfalls of a long-distance relationship, Eva was determined, in spite of her strong attraction to Peter, that her friendship with him would, without much effort, remain casual. Because she believed the intimacy between them would have geographical limits, Eva let her defenses down during her initial period of getting to know Peter. Peter, in turn, responded powerfully to this more relaxed, open version of Eva, and found plenty of excuses to visit her city.

Lulled by the safety of narrowed expectations, Eva saw in Peter qualities that she had never seen, or let herself see, in any other man. Intelligent and funny, with an unusual sensitivity and awareness of his own and other's feelings, Peter impressed her as someone for whom she could feel both affection and respect. The more time they spent together, the stronger her feelings became, and yet she remained satisfied that their physical distance would keep her from the terrifying demands of real, day-to-day intimacy.

So it was with a little delight and a lot of apprehension that Eva greeted Peter's news that he'd been offered a new and higher-level advocacy position by an organization located right in her city. It was one thing to be falling in love with someone who had the good manners to disappear via Amtrak every Sunday night and quite another to entertain the same arrangement on a full-time basis. But in spite of her reservations, she knew that, whatever the initial circumstances of their coming together, her emotional investment in Peter was more genuine and reciprocal than any she'd ever experienced. She realized that welcoming Peter into her real life could work to challenge the overly self-protective impulses that she now understood set significant limits on her ability to feel connected to another person.

It hasn't always been easy. Since Peter's move to her city, the two have grown closer and more committed, but in spite of the real happiness she feels with him, Eva has to work to keep her controlling impulses in check. Sometimes she's able to, and sometimes she's not, for the fear motivating her overcompensating behavior doesn't simply disappear once it's acknowledged.

The difference is that this time she's chosen someone to be involved with who is conscious enough to recognize what lies behind Eva's actions and is often able to defuse the moment of hypercontrol, rather than just respond to it blindly. Simple things, like raising an eyebrow in her direction when her voice tenses up or meeting her furrow-browed stare with a perfect imitation of it, can get her laughing at him—and herself. And as Eva continues to recognize that value of her union with Peter, she's able to see her own impulses more clearly and to short-circuit them. By placing her trust in someone who appreciates the significance of the gesture and returns it, Eva is slowly learning that closeness can exist even when she's not always in charge.

As with Eva, Susannah's love affair with control reveals a strong overcompensatory impulse, but Susannah isn't interested so much in controlling other people as she is in controlling herself. I met her many years ago, when she shared a suite in my younger sister's college dormitory. I'd recently had my heart unceremoniously broken by a callous young fellow and had traveled (by bus—never a good move for the recently dumped) to receive some sisterly succor. Said sister made the dubious decision to trundle me off to a party where the beverage of choice was pure-grain-alcohol punch. Consequently, she and Susannah were privy to the spectacle of an older, presumably more experienced woman badly disgracing herself in a public forum.

One look at Susannah and it's clear what the department stores had in mind when they cordoned off space for the petite section. She's a tiny little bug of a thing who lies herself up to five feet tall

and tips the scale at about ninety-five pounds. A gifted technophile
to whom the phrase *information superhighway* somehow does not
bring on thoughts of swallowing cyanide tablets and ending it all,
Susannah was snapped up, after graduating from college with every
conceivable honor, by one of those giant computer conglomerates
overflowing with well-compensated if deluded employees who
believe that the word *sexy* applies to efficient computer function.
Susannah spends her days designing ever more sophisticated programs to further advance the revenue of her already wealthy
company.

Susannah lives in a high-rise building whose oversized windows
offer magnificent views of Manhattan's East River and its various
seafaring vessels. The two floors of her spacious duplex apartment
are connected by a stainless steel circular staircase, and the highly
polished dark wood floors are bare but for throw rugs acquired during her extensive travels to the Far East. It's difficult to wander
through the perfectly appointed living room (with its bold and colorful artwork, its overstuffed antique-white furniture) or relax in the
kitchen (whose ingeniously designed cabinets hide any and all signs
of disarray and where rotting fruit is tossed away days before it's
had a chance to liquefy) and not begin to recognize the profound
inadequacy of one's own living arrangement. One begins to reevalu-
ate one's own prewar, fourth-floor walk-up tenement apartment—
which just hours ago seemed good enough to call home—as well
as to rethink the wisdom of using cardboard packing boxes as storage
space and furniture.

This is the thing about Susannah—good enough is not quite
good enough. For her, God is in the thread count, and one nap on
her billowy European goose-down comforter is all anyone would
need to find religion. She likes things just so, and has made it her
business to make sure they get and stay that way. And while it's easy
to envy the material excellence of her lifestyle—the exotic vacations,
the Donna Karan slip dresses and Manolo Blahnik strappy sandals,

the cleaning lady—it's also plain to see that Susannah has achieved her standards not through a windfall trust fund, but rather by sheer force of will.

While her work designing various parts of the software cosmos is demanding, and sometimes a bit rigid and confining, Susannah marches along uncomplainingly. Self-sufficiency is her goal, and she's attained it, never having to wonder if she can afford another beer while out with friends for drinks. She pays her rent, never charges groceries on her credit card, lays out her clothing the night before work. Suffice it to say that Susannah has never had to pay someone at H&R Block to fill out the EZ form of her tax return, nor has she ever, upon being told that she owed the government eight hundred dollars that she didn't have, spent several afternoon hours sitting on the floor of a crosstown bus, weeping.

But even as other people make a mockery of the word *adult*, Susannah's methods are extreme in their own way. While I'm all for retirement funds and tax shelters, it seems significant (even perhaps overcompensatory?) that someone would hurl themselves into a serious career at age twenty-one and simply stay there, never screwing up, never getting a hankering to chuck it all for a year and head out to Colorado to become a ski instructor or board a plane to Italy in pursuit of some appallingly gorgeous, mandolin-toting vagabond.

In dating, just as in life, Susannah's standard operating procedure leaves something to be desired in the spontaneity department. She approaches a date as though it were a job interview, remembering to have a suit dry-cleaned and to get a manicure. No one enjoys languishing in a sudsy bathtub for four or five hours in anticipation of a big night as much as I do, but pleasure is the last thing Susannah derives from her avant-date machinations. Pre-romance primping is the equivalent of getting her car tuned and gassed up—necessary, not something to get jazzed about.

And, indeed, getting jazzed about these men is the last thing Susannah is interested in when she's stepping into high heels. She wants dinner companionship, pleasant conversation, similar taste in movies. What she does not want is a grand passion. She tried that once, and it decidedly did not work out.

Susannah was one of those girls the experts might describe as slow to develop. She steered clear of the usual high school romances, and even in college was content to gaze admiringly—and from afar—at the captain of the football team or some equally inaccessible specimen. Unlike most of her friends, my sister included, who had begun hurling themselves at prospective boyfriends before the exhaust fumes from their parent's station wagons had dissipated, Susannah seemed peculiarly unmoved by the prospect of a campus overflowing with eligible bachelors. On those occasions when a member of the opposite sex seemed interested in her, she responded with such complete obtuseness that the interested party soon gave up in frustration.

Everything was going along swimmingly, if somewhat dully, until she met George. A sophisticated junior, George was a well-known fixture on campus. Head of the student body and captain of the rugby team, he seemed at twenty like a young Jack Kennedy without the back problems. With his good looks and plentiful charisma, it was understood that he could have any woman on campus. Although Susannah initially deflected his advances, once George had set his sights on her, it was only a matter of time before she had to acknowledge his interest. Soon enough, they were inseparable.

In love, Susannah transformed. Her cheeks were flushed with excited heat; everything delighted her. She adored George and was completely persuaded that he was her ideal companion. To her, George demonstrated none of the macho bravado that had characterized his public campus persona, revealing instead a side that was consistently thoughtful and tender. On those rare occasions that he was not by her side, Susannah sustained her girlish infatuation, blushing at the mention of his name, staring moonily at the photographs of the two that had accumulated on the bulletin board over her desk.

To the casual observer, this was a period of supreme happiness for Susannah. She'd held out for love, and it had arrived with none of the pettiness and mixed signals that characterized the romances her friends were forever falling in and out of. However, she claims that this period was one of considerable anxiety. "I was out of my mind with fear. It was entirely new, and I had no idea what was going to happen next." Perhaps her apprehension was due to the fact that, unbeknownst to us, clues of George's imminent defection were starting to surface.

When Susannah was able to maintain the reticence, the self-control for which she was known, George was wholly and perfectly consumed by his desire for her. But it's an old story and you've heard it before: The moment she began to reciprocate, to return the quality of attention George paid her, even at times to surpass it, George started to lose interest. Such a change is often not visible to the naked eye, but you feel it in your gut: Your poor stomach lurches as though you'd been dropped down an elevator shaft. And once you feel it, there's no turning back.

Once Susannah experienced the collapse of her organs, she knew instinctively that it was only a matter of time before her magical universe shattered. She worked hard to maintain her outward composure, desperate that George remain ignorant of her inner turmoil. George, sensing the increasing intensity of her attention, did what people who are being watched usually do; he tried to disappear.

Susannah's exaggerated composure, her very deliberate show of self-sufficiency (as Hirsch's good doctor would be quick to intuit) masked her feelings of tremendous, out-of-control need. And she had her reasons. When she was six years old, her mother died quite suddenly and painfully of cancer. As an only child, she had been particularly close to her mother, and while her father was well-intentioned and loving, his general cluelessness, combined with the fact that he'd been quite a bit older than her mother, made him a less-than-ideal substitute. And when Susannah was twelve, he died as well, of heart failure. She traveled to live with her mother's cousins, who were kind to her but who could never replicate the security she'd felt with her own parents. Relying on people and having them inexplicably disappear had convinced her that the only control she could hope to have lay in her complete independence.

And yet, having been so rudely relieved of protection and safety in her early life, Susannah craved the security and affirmation that George initially seemed prepared to provide. She worked hard to appear autonomous because she sensed her own neediness to be enormous. And she feared that the moment she let herself become truly vulnerable to another person, that vulnerability and the lack of safety it represented would translate into crushing disaster.

Which is precisely what happened. George hung around for a few months, increasingly cool in his response to Susannah's attentions, until a spicy little sophomore caught his eye and he vanished.

Susannah couldn't eat. She couldn't sleep. She couldn't drag herself out of bed to attend classes, she suffered from such violent panic attacks that she started taking Valium to control them. She began to look as shadowy and hollow-eyed as if she'd just stepped out of an Edvard Munch painting. She was convinced that George's defection was the result of some terrible, correctable misunderstanding. Because of her relative inexperience, Susannah did not realize she was witnessing the classic warrior's response to any conquest: After a quick survey of the carnage, the true soldier grabs his sword and hits the road, hungry for new challenges.

Susannah had overcome such enormous defenses in order to become close to George that, when he reneged on his part of the agreement, it seemed to her that she was completely exposed. And no matter how clear it was to everyone else that George was perfectly content in his new romantic dalliance, she immersed herself in the fantasy that she could undo what she somehow had done and get

George to love her again. No matter how awry things were, she believed that if she could just convince George that he'd been mistaken in leaving her, everything would instantly go back to normal.

To this deranged end, Susannah began to enact precisely the behavior that George had once employed to win her heart. She set her telephone on redial and called until he answered, she lingered outside his dorm entrance, she turned up outside his classes. To his discredit, as it was clear that reconciliation was not in the cards, George seemed to enjoy this attention, greeting Susannah with perverse friendliness as if it weren't the fifteenth time he'd run into her on a given day. Of course, his rampant sadism only encouraged her hopes, something everyone, including George, could plainly see. It wasn't until she happened to catch sight of him and his new inamorata working up a passionate sweat on the steps of the library that she was able to recognize the truth of the situation: George was a dog, and he was not a lonely one.

For a while things looked bleak. Susannah's roommates urged her to talk to them about how she was feeling or to consider seeing one of the counselors on campus, but Susannah seemed determined to handle her crisis on her own. Unlike Eva, who remained somewhat wary even during her happiest period with Sam, Susannah recognized that once the barriers were down, she had let herself be entirely swept away by her overwhelming need for love. Seeing this, she became determined not to allow that scenario to repeat itself. She gritted her teeth and pulled herself together, showing up once again at classes and arriving on schedule for her various jobs. Her determination was daunting and impressive, and it worked very effectively to reinforce her belief that to need anything at all was to set up oneself for heartbreak.

By the time her senior year drew to a close, Susannah seemed to have put the episode with George effectively behind her. While those around her coped with exams and senior theses and job interviews by swallowing Reese's Peanut Butter Cups whole and using their parents' American Express cards to call expensive psychic hot-lines, Susannah calmly purchased a conservatively cut charcoal gray suit and had her résumé printed onto bond paper. While her room-mates grimly practiced the phrase, "Would you like fries with that, sir?" and fantasized à la Lois Lane about careers in the low-paying "glamour" industries of journalism or advertising, Susannah showed up for meetings with the corporate representatives who were arriving in droves on the campus and left these meetings with actual job offers in hand. By the time graduation rolled around, Susannah was packing her bags for New York City.

Which is where she has remained, the overseer of an impres-sively consistent if not always completely thrilling life. And the truth is, Susannah is not a block of wood. There are times when she finds herself tempted to get closer to one of the men who pick her up for dinner at seven sharp and never spend the night. But, happily, change is in the air, for Susannah recently confessed that she'd experienced something of a close call with David, the stockbroker whose company she's been occasionally keeping.

"When I told him I wanted our relationship to stay casual, I thought he was going to get mad. Instead, he did the funniest thing—he told me he wanted to take me ice skating. I thought that was kind of sweet," she explained, blushing becomingly. "I hadn't been in years and was falling all over myself and him. But he was so nice about it, like he really didn't mind being pinned across the ice under my full weight. And then, afterward, we went out for mulled wine, and even though I was exhausted, I also felt great. And when he leaned over and kissed me, I felt like saying, 'Let's get out of here,' and going home to my place."

"So, did you?" I asked, my fingers crossed like pretzels.

"Oh, no. I couldn't. But I wanted to. Which I think he knew."

"When will you see him again?" I inquired, ever hopeful.

"Actually, he's coming by tomorrow. He says he wants to stay in and rent a movie. Do you think I should be worried?"

I lyingly assured her that I was certain David had nothing in mind but cinematic pleasures and hung up the phone, optimistic that Susannah's friend, if he was as thoughtful and perceptive as he sounded, would be vigilant in his efforts to prove to her that the absence of control, in small doses, could be an entirely good thing.

Controlled is the last word you'd be tempted to use to describe Maggie. Her usual plan is to not have a plan, to let the day take her wherever it likes and never to allow unexpected developments to derail the party train. Her apartment is small and sparsely decorated, giving the impression that its owner has just taken up residence and not yet gotten around to unpacking. But this suits Maggie, as she needs the space that, say, furniture would take up to accommodate the constant influx of partyers and unannounced overnight guests. Maggie rolls languorously out of bed each morning, stepping calmly over whichever bodies happen to be resting on her floor, and shuffles into the kitchen to make coffee. Usually these guests are suffering from hangovers or recovering from some chemically induced solitary fiesta, but Maggie takes this in stride, methodically pouring orange juice into shatterproof glasses and making neat little rows of B-complex vitamins and Aleve caplets.

Living in Los Angeles, Maggie is every ounce the peroxide-happy California girl, from her perpetual tan to her Victoria's Secret figure. She works as a publicist for a giant record company, arranging interviews and tours for and managing the public image of a great coven of guitar-toting, skeletally thin recording stars. Maggie is one of those curious individuals who actually like to keep busy, and she especially likes it if keeping busy entails attending dozens of high-profile parties and flying across the country to attend rock concerts.

Maggie does a lot of traveling for her work, and her trips are usually a frenzy of cocktail parties and expense-account dinners. Though she is often forced to socialize with complete strangers, she does not, like some of us, feel compelled to take refuge from these gatherings in a ladies' room stall, obsessively examining her incipient crow's feet and ever-widening pores in the mirror of her Clinique compact. No, sir—Maggie remains firmly in the party's epicenter, laughing gaily at the bon mots of record producers and grunge musicians. Maggie's a wild child, and wild children tend not to put much stock in self-consciousness.

Although professional ascension is another thing Maggie tends not to put much stock in, she's generally well liked at work. This is partly because of her genial good nature, and partly because she happens to be packaged so attractively. This latter is not a small detail when it comes to pleasing her company's particular clientele—ask Heather Locklear. Maggie is the ultimate optimist who manages to turn the most appalling events into excellent stories, usually at her own expense.

Unlike most of her friends, Maggie tends to be fairly tame regarding vices—cigarettes, or an occasional glass of wine too many—except, naturally, when it comes to men. She can smell trouble when it walks into the room, and it's a scent that appeals to her. In the time since I've known her, she's been involved with three men: a Ferrari-driving sales rep for the cocaine industry, a dyed-in-the-wool and utterly charming alcoholic, and a bass player with an appetite for psychotropic self-medication so insatiable that his mere existence seems to answer the question of whether reincarnation is possible, as well as solving the mystery of Ur-rocker Jim Morrison's whereabouts.

As a rule, these men are difficult to manage, and it's clear that Maggie takes a certain pride in her ability to manage them. Though she acknowledges that her paramours are definitely high-maintenance, she enters each new relationship rapturously innocent of the trouble ahead. But once again, if we look at her behavior with the seasoned skepticism of our favorite cinematic analyst, it becomes clear that Maggie's "innocence" of all manner of ominous romantic signposts is very deliberately cultivated. After all, whole schools of psychological thought have been built around the concept that even the lowliest laboratory rat is capable of learning from its mistakes.

Maggie's pattern in these entanglements is always the same. The very snarly, criminal qualities that eventually prove troubling are what initially attract her to each new conquest. The can't-pin-me-down-because-I'm-dangerous swagger, the menacingly seductive stare, the pomade—all spell romance to Maggie. She could get normal guys; with her sweet conviviality and long, white-blond hair, she could probably get Antonio Banderas. Friends have tried to pry her away from type, dragging her to parties or dinners to meet more appropriate potential suitors. The men she meets like Maggie; they call her up and ask her on dates that she doesn't even bother lying to avoid. She hangs up the phone, mortified, muttering, "Loser!" under her breath, then settles in for an evening of watching *Cops*, just on the off chance that she'll catch a glimpse of her latest beau, drunk and stripped down to his underwear, bent over the hood of a car while several members of the LAPD fit him with a pair of handcuffs.

Maggie's laissez-faire attitude changes somewhat dramatically, however, the moment she develops an actual attachment to one of these men. This shift is marked by a sudden and passionate engagement in her partner's potential rehabilitation. The transition from cheerleader to rehab counselor creates a conflict that Maggie experiences as profound discomfort, so invested is she in her role as permission giver, as enhancer rather than inhibitor of any sort of pleasure. Although she needs to sustain belief in her own liberal-mindedness, the truth is that Maggie has fairly conventional and familiar expectations of devotion and accountability when it comes to love. Once she's truly involved, she invests a tremendous amount of energy in negotiating the chasm between supporter and detractor of the man in her life, alternately criticizing and defending this person's behavior both to herself and to the world outside the relationship. Inevitably, though, she is forced to conclude that, however appealing the bad-boy antics of her current beau once were to her, she can no longer tolerate finishing such a poor second to his other, more demanding and illegal priorities.

During the denouement of her affair with Cap, the bass player, Maggie decided to take a break from the relationship and spend a couple of days at my apartment. I had been experiencing my own troubles in love, having realized that my then-boyfriend was spending altogether too much time with a coworker. Though I was fairly sure that this friendship was still platonic—the two shared some genuine interests, and the woman appeared to be happily involved in her own relationship—I had succumbed to a certain level of irrational and decidedly unattractive jealousy. I was pleased at the thought of a visit and hoped that Maggie's company would distract me from my own very likely self-created problems.

Maggie arrived, and we immediately started in on some girl talk. I handed her a pint of Vanilla Swiss Almond, grabbed a container of Chocolate Chip Cookie Dough (a flavor that shouldn't work, but somehow does) for myself, and settled in to listen. Things had taken a clearly disastrous turn with Cap—something having to do with his recent theft and demolition of her automobile—though Maggie was not quite at the point where she could admit failure. Eventually, she grew tired of talking and persuaded me to share my own sad tale. I was somewhat reluctant even to waste her time, as I knew the problem was largely of my own invention, but I went ahead and recounted some of my concerns about my beau. Maggie listened sympathetically and, when I finished, proceeded to reassure me that my fears were unfounded, thoughtfully coming up with examples of my boyfriend's fidelity that had not occurred to me. I was grateful for this and felt reassured that the problem was all in my head.

Our conversation then returned to the minutiae of Maggie's relations with Cap. Even as she detailed his misbehavior, I noticed that Maggie was careful to praise Cap for those redeeming qualities she could still locate. As it was so plainly obvious to me that Cap was nothing more than a bass-playing goon and that Maggie would be lucky if the destruction of her Sentra was the extent of the damage this relationship would wreak, I began—delicately, as only a girlfriend can—to explore the possibility of her calling off the affair. As I began to list the reasons for her doing so, the arguments were so strong that I lost sight of my diplomacy. I became determined to make it clear to Maggie that she deserved more than she was getting from Cap, and rather impolitically attempted to make her see that Cap was an unmitigated loser who was never going to change his stripes.

Deep into my pint of premium ice cream and enjoying my own tirade, I neglected to glance up at Maggie's face. When I did, I was surprised to see that it was white with fury, her lovely lips pulled tight in a terrifying grimace. I braced myself for what was coming, suddenly aware that I had gone too far. "Well," Maggie said coolly, leaning back against the couch cushions. "Cap may be difficult at times. But at least I know he isn't making an ass of me by cheating." The "which is more than you can say" hung heavily and miserably in the air.

Okay, my feelings were definitely hurt. But in spite of myself, I was intrigued by the rare view into Maggie's heart that her indiscretion offered. In a Judd Hirsch instant, I saw that she was furious— at me, just then, yes, but also in general. Underneath the sunny, accepting exterior, Maggie was ready to explode. And, seeing this, what had been so previously puzzling became absolutely clear: Maggie's persistent attraction to angry malcontents was her way of managing her own anger.

By choosing men who engage in all manner of destructive and irresponsible activity, Maggie can inhabit by proxy the impulses toward rebellion and churlishness that she otherwise keeps deep underground. In order to overcompensate for the troubling, malignant feelings brewing beneath her surface, she has cultivated an image of ferociously sustained gaiety. But the truth will out, as our mothers warned us, and while Maggie is usually able to contain her own darker side, such a side effectively reveals itself in her choice of partners.

Maggie's wild lifestyle exists in direct contrast to her deep southern upbringing. She was raised in central Texas by parents for whom the appearance of propriety was tantamount in importance to breathing (her father was a minister; her mother, a dutiful, long-suffering minister's wife), and the lessons of her childhood seem to have convinced her that such unseemly emotions as rage and discontent are completely unacceptable, especially for nice girls from Texas. The aftereffects of her good-girl upbringing continue to profoundly affect her romantic life. If Maggie could express, or even accept, her angry side, chances are she wouldn't have to find men to do it for her. She might be able to get involved with a man who could offer her something beyond an opportunity to pay his bail.

Unfortunately, Maggie is galaxies away from acknowledging her darker side, let alone attempting to integrate it into her self-concept. Emboldened by my Hirschian insight, I decided to ask Maggie to talk about the truculent remark she made about my romantic situation. I told her, "It's okay, I know you were angry at me. I was being an obnoxious nightmare. Let's just talk about it." Rather than being relieved at the chance to voice her irritation, Maggie frantically attempted to assure me that I was mistaken, that she hadn't meant her comment to be hostile. She had been merely pointing out one good quality of Cap's; surely I could see that? Well, what I saw was her reconciliation with Cap, and the months ahead of wasted time as she allowed her wayward boyfriend to give voice to what, for Maggie, remained unspeakable.

Yes, dear reader, in times such as these, one longs for the clear-eyed and reassuring presence of the good doctor Hirsch. Judd could peel away the armor we've constructed around ourselves, revealing to us those qualities we've tried unsuccessfully to reject. He would gently guide us toward accepting those parts of ourselves that we've tried so hard and in vain to deny, because Judd knows that ignoring an aspect of oneself doesn't make it disappear. It just makes achieving any level of complete self-acceptance impossible.

Judd would remind us, at a very reasonable hourly rate, that until we can face ourselves wholly and honestly, intimacy with another person will remain a pipe dream. He would point out that even if we do find someone to love the self we present, rather than the actual, fully integrated person we are, such love will feel hollow and unsatisfying, for it will have been inspired by a person who does not exist.

It's an old truth, but nonetheless a valid one: In our culture, women feel a tremendous pressure to conform to a certain ideal of good behavior—to be pleasant and undemanding, to control our inclination toward neediness or anger, to be, at all costs, reasonable. Unfortunately, this pressure does not bear much relationship to the fact that, as humans, we contain the whole spectrum of emotions and impulses, from euphoria to misery, contentment to rage. It's a fantasy to think, as Maggie certainly does, that we can regulate our internal selves; by attempting to do so, all we do is get ourselves into trouble and reinforce our feelings of shame and unworthiness, feelings that can take all the fun out of an expensive candlelit dinner for two.

A person out of touch with the reality of who she is cannot possibly make herself available for a genuine and committed relationship. Before one can think of achieving communion with another, one must first experience such communion with oneself. For these women, it's going to mean taking a hard look at areas of compulsiveness in their lives and determining what this behavior is attempting to mask. But the answer, as our pal Conrad comes to understand, will be far less frightening than the unacknowledged shadowland of horrors that keeps us far away from fulfilling emotional connections. And once we begin to see ourselves fully, we can also begin the substantial process of revealing that self to others.

7

A Pound of Flesh

How Female Commitment-Phobes Make Bathing Suit Anxiety Work for Us

I REMEMBER QUITE CLEARLY my first Weight Watchers meeting. The large, flourescent-lit room lined with rows of folding chairs, the discreet screen behind which loomed a black, brooding doctor's scale—an arrangement reminiscent of that of the Great and Powerful Oz. We fatties paid for the privilege of lining up and being weighed by suspiciously thin group leaders who provided a pantomimed reaction to our weekly progress: happy face for weight loss, sad for gain, grim commiseration if we stayed the same. Theirs was a kind of salaried tolerance, a vigilant empathy that affirmed the principle about which we had come to be reminded: the concomitant shame and exoneration inherent in group weight rituals. This collective, highly public monitoring seemed to owe something to the Catholic sacrament of confession, which I was beginning to hear about in my catechism class, being, at that time, all of nine years old.

So it is with some authority that I say I cannot imagine that there's a woman alive who has not suffered over her appearance. While our culture is content to judge men in terms of superior intellect or ambition, when it comes to estimating a woman's value, the salient considerations seem to be (a) can she suck it into a size 6? (b) has she, by means of luck or chemical peel or a life spent under a parasol, retained a wrinkle-free and radiant complexion? and (c) has she managed—against all odds, considering the legions of hair terrorists lurking everywhere—to find a stylist who can do something with that unruly mane of hers?

Women are taught to regard their physical characteristics as essential currency in the marketplace of love. Which means that if we happen to draw a bum hand in the genetic poker game and end up with frizzy hair or a prominent nose or hips, we might as well kiss any hope of love goodbye. While on some level we may know that attraction is subjective—that our potential mate may actually like the fact that we wear glasses—all we have to do is tune into *Melrose Place* to be reminded that our thighs are too heavy or our chin is all wrong and, really, just who are we trying to kid?

Because the culture puts so much emphasis on a woman's looks, it's almost inevitable that our feelings about our appearance (anxiety, pride, proud anxiety) will have a direct impact on the manner in which we conduct ourselves in the world. Our relationships with our families and friends, our professional behavior, our romantic encounters—all are affected by the shame or confidence or desolation with which we regard our own physical incarnation.

And when we're uneasy about commitment, or the intimacy that necessarily precedes it, it's only logical that we rely on our bodies to express this discomfort. It works something like this: We figure out the conventional standard of female physical perfection (issues of *Allure* magazine or episodes of MTV's Cindy Crawford vehicle, *House of Style,* are convenient Monarch Notes to this lesson), we ascertain the degree to which our own gene pool has cooperated with this model, and then we set about adapting our natural aspect as much as humanly possible to this standard of beauty. That's one version.

However, if you're eager to avoid romantic involvement and

are looking for an easy way out of it, the existence of this sanctified female ideal offers you something concrete to rebel against. Such rebellion can take many forms: gaining weight, failing to purchase contact lenses, neglecting the upkeep of your roots (unless you happen to be Heather Locklear, who succeeds somehow in pulling off the reverse-skunk look), dressing like a Carmelite novitiate about to take her final vows. By taking any or all of these actions, a woman is free to blame her single state on her flawed appearance and effectively avoid consideration of the more troubling possibility that maybe she'd simply rather be on her own. Said woman certainly has the culture's full cooperation in this perception, as any dissension from the female ideal is swiftly deemed a deliberate and bad-tempered act of secession. And if you're busy seceding, you're not busy dating.

Now, I know there are plenty of women for whom, because of heredity or medical conditions or because they have problems of such a pressing nature that they just don't have time to join Jenny Craig, this standard of physical perfection is an impossibility. Which doesn't even touch those women who consider the mere thought of such standards pure nonsense worthy only of derision and dismissal. But those wise souls are the exception; most of us do buy into the notion that the failure to come up to snuff fairly ensures our romantic liberty. Such failure to make the grade also guarantees us a considerable amount of misery, because, in general, our society is much nicer to the flawless physical specimens than it is to the flawed. It just likes them better, is all. Nothing personal intended.

And, really, in an ideal universe, no offense would be taken, for how could we possibly be offended by a set of standards that have absolutely nothing to do with us? The conviction that the sum of women's physical parts is exactly equal to our whole is unbelievably boring and depressing. Unfortunately, it's a conviction that encourages us to lose all sight of what is reasonable and just in the world as we find ourself capitulating—sometimes actively, sometimes as if we've been tossed off the side of a building—to the peculiar notion that physical perfection translates, for women, into moral virtue. Which leads us (whether our lineaments correspond to the current, evanescent standards of comeliness or not) to indulge in a relentless and highly toxic critique of our exterior selves that removes the focus of our self-analysis from where it belongs: under our skin.

If you find yourself locked in the grip of physical self-loathing (however understandable, thanks to Kate Moss and the proof she offers that God is, indeed, mocking us) and attributing your romantic Hindenbergs to the inadequacy of your appearance, there's an excellent chance that you're unwittingly using your body as a passport out of the nation of romantic commitment. It's the conviction we feel concerning our so-called physical inadequacies and the manner in which this conviction warps our behavior, rather than the shortcomings themselves, that impede romantic progress.

I can still recall the first holiday season I passed with my current beau. We spent several festive, snowy days indulging in the usual bacchanalia of fruitcake and buttery chestnut stuffing, then returned home laden with bags of gifts and the traditional food hangovers. My beloved leapt up early the following morning, prepared to resume normal life, and pulled on a pair of jeans. "Hey," he exclaimed, his voice filled with wonderment, "I think I've gained some weight."

I was astounded. This development was, to him, a completely neutral one, the emotional equivalent of noticing that a light bulb has burned out and needs replacing. Where was the shame, the guilt, the nightmare of self-damnation? I had put on weight myself— who wouldn't have, subsisting almost exclusively for five days on a diet of heavy cream? But this realization kept me trapped beneath the covers, preparing to spend the day clutching my rounded stomach and weeping, taking an hourly mental inventory of the clothes hanging in my closet that would no longer fit me. What was for him an interesting fact to take note of, perhaps to address with a few days of lighter eating, was for me a moral indictment from which there was no possible salvation. The change in my beau's body had occurred externally, separate from his self, whereas for me it had the power to define my essential worth or, more accurately, lack thereof.

Of course, I had learned early on about the universal revilement of extra flesh, when a childhood illness and the attendant period of bed rest (about which I was privately joyous, given the weeks of grueling and disagreeable outdoor play from which I was saved) left me a bit zaftig. Upon recovering, I returned to school and ran smack into my one of my favorite teachers, a gruff old guy with a sharp sense of humor. "Sheila," he greeted me loudly. "You got so big!"

This was possibly the first time I understood that one's body could take a serious wrong turn, as mine obviously had by getting larger. This information, which would be amplified in all manner of ways as I got older, was of critical importance to me. Not only did it suggest to me precisely the manner in which I could easily reinforce the poor self-image I was already developing, but it would also offer me an escape route in later years when I was looking for a passive way to deflect romantic involvement.

Like most women, my relationship with my weight was and is more complicated than an inherited predisposition for child-bearing hips or the wholesale availability of pound cake in my mother's cabinets (although I can't say that these factors were exactly deterrents, either). Because we live in a society that hates fat, carrying excess weight can be an amazingly effective method of ensuring one's own isolation. The metaphor of extra padding couldn't be more apt: Padding offers protection. Unfortunately, its presence can also guarantee a certain exclusion from some fairly important experiences. Interaction with the opposite sex, for example, tends to fall by the wayside, as does any semblance of ease with one's own body. Given that in our flesh-hating culture, excess weight is a guaranteed target for criticism, heaviness can act as an effective camouflage for more worrying fears having to do with such substantive considerations as personality or character.

In my case, the cycle of weight loss and weight gain was a constant companion until I reached my middle twenties. And whether I was in a period of relative fatness or thinness, I thought of myself as huge. My self-image communicated itself quite clearly to any prospective suitors: Being heavy is a pretty good talisman against romantic success, but there's no doubt that I exacerbated an already bad situation with my exceedingly negative self-image. Objectively, of course, the issue of how much or little one weighs has nothing to do with her worth as a person. But then again, there was nothing objective about weight for me. I had no idea—until I started therapy and began to excavate the painful assumptions I'd made about myself as a child—the extent to which I had been relying on the very thing I most detested about myself, my extra weight, to relay to the world the extent of my unworthiness. During my lengthy and difficult (and far-from-finished) process of gaining self-knowledge and acceptance, I've come to see how my weight has acted as a guard against my fears and frustration regarding intimacy and close-ness with other people. I had the culture's complete cooperation in this process, to be sure, but the heavy-duty work of keeping myself buried under that pound of flesh was my own and was suited per-fectly to my self-isolating purposes.

When I met my better half, several years ago, I happened to be at a weight that was for me quite low. I had just concluded what was perhaps the world's unhealthiest weight reduction plan—one of my own devising, I hasten to add. It consisted of half a dry bagel in the morning, followed by a cup of pasta at dinner. If I went out for an evening on the town, I'd skip dinner and stick to straight vodka, which, as anyone who owns a scale knows, is the lowest-calorie alcoholic beverage available. I do not recommend this diet, which was plainly the brainchild of a psychotic mind, but for a brief period it did the trick. Fortunately, this diet worked without the aid of physical exercise (one of the requirements of a good diet, in my book), and this was a lucky thing, for even standing up too quickly proved a bit too tasking during this period of asceticism.

In any event, once I fell in love, all that ended. The man of my dreams was an enthusiastic cook and an equally enthusiastic eater. Immersed in the throes of my newly paired state, I became a metabolism amnesiac, the victim of a dietary fugue. I simply forgot that washing down huge plates of lasagna with countless glasses of red wine would have an adverse effect on my figure. For a few months I indulged in a dangerous combination of ecstatic abandon and serious compulsiveness, until the morning I awakened to face the fact that, like bread set out to rise, I was rapidly doubling in bulk.

Denial being what it is, I refused to consider my weight increase in any terms other than the radical change in my diet. If my beloved set a heaping plate of potato au gratin before me, gloriously combining food and love, who was I to refuse it? As the months passed and I gradually began exchanging one wardrobe for, shall we say, a roomier one, I steadfastly ignored the all-too-familiar motif having to do with overeating as a path to self-loathing and isolation. That's right, friends, things were getting a little too serious, a little too intimate, with my beau, and what better way to make him to jump ship, to get him to leave me rather than having to take any action myself, than by turning into the nineties' version of Totie Fields?

I would probably still be ignoring my knee-jerk reaction to intimacy and weighing in at a solid three hundred pounds if my boyfriend hadn't forced me to own up to my behavior. Terrifying, but true: He confronted me about my weight gain. Now, having one's fellow point out one's widening girth is not exactly the stuff of which fantasies are made, and the first time my beau gingerly broached the subject I believe I screamed something along the lines of, "I hope you burn in hell!" before fleeing the room in tears.

It took me a long time before I could discuss this topic with any semblance of rationality. But my boyfriend kept at it, until I finally saw that, while interested in the changes occurring in my body, he did not share my nightmarish associations with weight gain. He was not interested in judgment or recrimination but rather, knowing something of my history of using my body as a weapon against closeness with others, was concerned about the implications the changes he was witnessing might have for our increasing commitment. Before this encounter, I'd believed my disinclination to discuss matters of weight represented my hard-earned recovery of the right to privacy and dominion over my body. And it's true that such control is hugely important to me. However, what I eventually also realized was that my boyfriend wanted not to control my body but rather to subvert my inclination to protect and sustain my negative feelings about myself and thus allow those feelings to act as a deterrent to our communion.

Weight continues to be an issue for me and, given my history, it likely always will be. I continue to spend an inordinate amount of time contemplating my own physical inadequacies; I care too much about the fact that I will never be able to wear those ridiculously sexy thigh-high stockings with a miniskirt; I can lose whole days to thoughts of what I have or haven't eaten. I don't know if I'll ever be able to say to myself, "A body is just a vessel," and mean it. For now, the best I can do is try to understand the nature of this obsession and to try to monitor its effect on me. The inclination to disappear into my solitary, fleshy self has not vanished, but my growing understanding of the problem and my increasing ability to share it with those close to me—in particular with my mate—go a long way toward diffusing the alienation that is, for me, the downside of the food equation.

I've known Lila for almost three decades. When I was five and about to begin kindergarten, my family bought a house down the road from hers. On the first day of school, Lila and I stood on my front lawn while my mother, squinting through her vale of tears, snapped Polaroids of us before trundling us off to experience formal education. At age five, Lila was a curly-headed, sweet-faced little girl, extremely gregarious and sunny. It was easy to see that she was interested in pleasing the people around her. But even at that young age, there was a definite anxiety underlying her desire to be liked and accepted.

Lila was a child of unusual intelligence, and she lived in a home where such qualities were valued. Though her parents had, for professional reasons, moved to the bucolic suburban area where we lived, they did not abandon their urban sensibilities. And they were determined that their children be raised with the same level of cultural sophistication that they themselves had been raised with — a somewhat unusual goal among the families in our area, and one that encouraged Lila's natural precocity.

Whereas my home was decidedly child-oriented, with whole rooms devoted to the architecture of Barbie villages and Byzantine couch-cushion forts, Lila's house revolved around adult pleasures. To me, a visit to Lila's was exotic and interesting: Mozart on the stereo, unpronounceable and complicated French delicacies at dinner, punctuated by sips of her parents' wine. But it could be a rigid place, too, with elaborate guidelines regarding which possessions could and could not be touched, the volume of our voices, even subtle hints about which games were appropriate and which were better avoided.

While Lila no doubt eventually came to appreciate and even share her parents' aesthetic, as a little girl she was drawn to a more child-friendly environment. Which was where my family came in. In our house, junk food and television were the ruling monarchy, a form of government Lila very quickly intuited as benevolent. Every afternoon, like clockwork, her curly red head appeared at our front door. As my mother had made the dubious decision to fill an entire kitchen cabinet with a bounty of delicacies from Hostess and Sara Lee, Lila had plenty of opportunity to fortify herself before joining me in the den to spend an afternoon watching reruns of *Marcus Welby, M.D.* and *The Brady Bunch.*

Even as a child, it was clear to me that there was trouble in Lila's paradise. Her father was a brilliant, difficult man who seemed determined that his children conform to a demanding set of expectations that often appeared to have little relation to their actual young ages. One result of Lila's precocity was that she demonstrated at an early age an independent and strong will, and probably because of this, her father's attention—and scorn—fell most frequently upon her. Lila's mother, a far more sympathetic soul, attempted to mitigate the conflict between her husband and her oldest daughter, but the two seemed destined to butt heads.

One of Lila's most appealing qualities is her abundant appetite: for sensual pleasure, for close friendship, for intellectual and aesthetic stimulation. She talks, eats, reads with voluptuous intensity. This healthy appetite has been a part of her during all the years I've known her and was probably present at birth. And, to an overly controlling parent, Lila's zest for experience presented itself as the perfect weapon for control.

Shortly after I met Lila, she made it clear to me that she thought she was fat. She was forever being put on strict, rigidly healthful diets and having her weight closely (I would say cruelly) monitored. In the photographs I have from that time, featuring Lila and me decked out in our watch-plaid first-day-of-school dresses, Lila looks perfect: solid and healthy, still a bit rounded with baby fat, pretty much identical to me. And yet my memories of this time are of Lila's constant anxiety and yearning about food, the palpable sense of prohibition that accompanied every bite she consumed. Her daily exodus to my mother's snack cabinet revealed an already formed compulsion to resist the police-state attitude about eating that her father did everything he could to enforce.

Once Lila had mastered the principles of longing and deprivation in the food lesson, she decided to apply this model to love. Although from age five or six Lila and I and all our girlfriends were completely fixated on our male schoolmates, desperate for some sign of attention or acceptance from them, Lila sought greater challenges, choosing without fail the most adorable, most popular, and least available boy as her object of affection, though it goes without saying that there really weren't any available boys in the first grade. Nevertheless, Lila seemed particularly bent on sustained yearning, for the boys she chased were far too concerned with advancing their own popularity (often accomplished with sadistic behavior toward their female classmates) to be interested in even a schoolyard friendship.

Eventually, and not unexpectedly, Lila's father's fantasy about his daughter's weight problem began to become a reality. This man was so committed to his belief that Lila was overweight that she, being a dutiful daughter, had little choice but to comply. Additionally, through his attitude, food had become such an impossibly tantalizing entity that there wasn't much Lila could do to resist it. It didn't help that Lila's mother, even while she acted as referee in the feud between her husband and daughter, was engaged in her own rather consuming struggle with weight maintenance.

As a kind of general rule, women tend to hate their own excess weight, and men prefer to loathe the excess weight of others—in particular, female others. Tiny men must be handed index cards upon emergence from the womb with the instructions, "Remember: Fat is the devil's Play-Doh," or some similar message. When we were children, my brother and I both considered chocolate-chip ice cream our primary reason for living. I can remember the two of us sitting at the kitchen table in something of a showdown—I, polishing off a half-gallon of the stuff, he, sublimating his craving by eating five peaches, one after the other. He was trying to teach by example the rudiments of discipline and self-control, but sadly, I was a very disappointing pupil. He's probably out running his daily five miles right now, planning to reward himself on his arrival home with a big, juicy, irresistible piece of fruit.

But back to Lila, whose particular experience with the body was made especially difficult, as the two things she most craved, food and love, virtually cancelled out the possibility for satisfaction in the other. And Lila exacerbated an already bad situation by continuing to fixate on the playground's versions of Brad Pitt, boys who didn't know she was alive. Through elementary school and high school, even into college, the men she liked were without fail the most stunning and unapproachable specimens around. Lila compensated in what is to many of us an exceedingly familiar way—she became an indispensible confidante and platonic friend. She supplicated herself rather dishearteningly to the guys she liked, exercising sufficiently poor judgment to even act as envoy between the men she adored and their current crushes, inevitably golden-haired cheerleaders or high school versions of the runway model.

Like me, Lila has spent most of her life on a diet or thinking about being on a diet. Months may go by between our phone conversations, yet five minutes into the call we're reciting our daily food intake for the other's approval. Regardless of which of us has currently decided to eschew once and for all the futility of dieting, all the other has to do is whisper one well-chosen phrase (*bathing suit*, for example, or *fat-free sour cream*), and we're off. We share an encyclopedic knowledge of organized reducing plans, whether Weight Watchers (the only marginally sane diet), Diet Center (based on the food plans developed in Dachau), or the hardcore panic button of diets (usually contemplated a month or two before the warm weather kicks in), Slim-Fast. We've embraced and summarily rejected every fad diet reprinted in women's magazines or published in book form. We've suffered through the headaches, the racing hearts, the faintness, the—God help me—recidivism. Though we decidedly are not now, we have both been thin.

And because we have both been thin, we know that being so doesn't make the world's problems, or our own within that world, magically disappear. We can even go so far, during our rare moments of lucidity, to admit that sometimes it's kind of a relief to be able to attribute one's troubles to our metabolically dead (murdered, really, by ourselves) bodies. We even know that there are prospective partners out there who either reject the general cultural detestation of large bodies or even prefer flesh to bone. (I've experienced this latter firsthand, actually, as I once briefly dated a man—very attractive, sort of a Jewish Mel Gibson, and a physician, to boot—who made the halting announcement to me during our third or fourth date that while he liked me very much, he didn't see the relationship going any further. When I inquired as to why he felt this way— we'd been getting along wonderfully—he muttered something about physical attraction. I slid miserably down into my chair, my eyes searching for the nearest exit, but my companion ignored my distress and continued. The problem, it seemed, was my weight. The stuff of every woman's nightmares, yes? So you can imagine my surprise when he went on to explain that I just wasn't heavy enough for his taste. Talk about a whole new frontier, fantasy-wise. Think of it— second, even third helpings, all in the name of keeping one's man interested. Sadly, this particular fellow did not have sufficient confidence in my weight-gaining abilities. Had he hung around for a few months, I could have showed him a thing or two about French fries and gravy. But, however lovingly, I do digress.)

Lila has made something of a career of ferreting out those men who do not share the predilections of this particular gentleman who got away (and took with him all my dreams about whipping cream). Obviously, good looks are subjective, and in a perfect world none of us would ever be judged by her appearance, conventionally attractive or not. But when we find ourselves consistently drawn to men who seem to have stepped fully formed out of a Ralph Lauren ad, not only are we practicing the same objectification of which men are routinely accused, but we are very likely also setting up elaborate obstacles to romantic fulfillment. The men whom Lila liked weren't just great-looking, they were men who rejoiced in physical perfection, from their cosmetically bonded smiles all the way down to their peach-tart buttocks. They didn't have time for Lila, with her razor-sharp intelligence and raucous sense of humor—they had to get to the gym.

By consistently choosing to fall for men who were already deeply in love with themselves, Lila was guaranteeing herself a safe distance from intimacy. It's not difficult to imagine why she feared true engagement with a man. Her first experience of male intimacy was not only punishing but also had as its primary objective the control and censorship of her individuality. By fostering obsessive crushes on unattainable—or, more recently, merely inappropriate—men, Lila can enjoy the bittersweet sensations of a love affair while retaining her emotional independence.

Lila's been involved for over two years now with a man named Ken. About a year before meeting him, she embarked on a personal transformation campaign, subsisting on a diet of broccoli and ice water, training like a decathlon athlete, and generally exploring the boundaries of manic compulsiveness. She bought herself a short skirt and a pair of heels, wore bright red lipstick, got herself a tan. So when Ken began to openly pursue her, Lila felt that her extreme efforts had been vindicated.

Ken was different from most of the men in whom she had previously been interested. Huge and muscle-bound, he had worked for several years in construction before starting his own contracting business. His passions—beer, televised sporting events, beer—struck her as irresistibly exotic and manly, much as his physical bulk made Lila feel as tiny and delicate as a little flower. She was entranced.

Ken had very specific ideas about division of labor within a relationship, and these ideas went roughly as follows: men go to work, women to go to work and do everything else. At first it was kind of amusing to watch Lila try her hand at playing wife—poring over cookbooks, gazing at Ken as he bolted down her latest culinary triumph, jumping up to clear away his plate or freshen his drink. Later, this posture of servitude seemed much less amusing and just plain strange. What was Lila, who could speak at least four languages fluently and hold her own in a debate about everything from Serbo-Croatian politics to the early works of Caravaggio, doing playing scullery maid to this neck-free endomorph?

Perhaps Lila was wondering this very same thing, but having spent so much of her life dreaming of a real romantic partnership, who was she to complain? Of course, the little voice in Lila that was always quick to say, "this is bullshit," hadn't exactly disappeared; it was just lying low for a while. Caught in the age-old commitment-phobic dilemma of deciding whether nothing is better than something, Lila turned for answers to the one thing that had always been there for her in the past: her refrigerator. She started eating. With each Twinkie, she found solace and pleasure, as well as the peace of knowing that before long Ken would tire of her widening waistline and move on to thinner pastures.

Unfortunately, while Ken wasn't exactly delirious about the changes in Lila's figure, he wasn't all that anxious to take his leave. Would you be quick to relinquish an arrangement that kept you beautifully fed and cared for, that required nothing of you but sustained breathing? Which tossed the ball right back into Lila's court—and she knew it.

"Why should he leave?" she asked resignedly, during our last phone conversation. "He's got it made here. I know it's up to me to make the break, but I'm completely paralyzed." She paused for a long moment. "What if I never find anyone else?"

Although she won't remain so forever, right now Lila's stuck. She's relatively safe with Ken; she knows he's not capable of fathoming the subtle nuances of her soul. She also recognizes that the chances of happiness with him are about as unlikely as getting through a week on Slim-Fast without a migraine. Lila wants love, but not at the price of her own identity. It's her own distinctive voice she wants to keep on hearing, rather than someone else's instructions about who she should be. Unfortunately, she doesn't yet believe that there are relationships in which her own voice would be seen not as an expression of correctable disobedience but as a welcome, essential component. The day she starts to believe such a partnership is possible, she'll toss her apron into the fireplace, pick up the telephone, and start ordering out.

Because to be overweight is a culturally sanctioned handicap, as Lila and I have learned, being so can act as a kind of shorthand for women who wish to communicate their disinclination toward intimacy with others. But what about those women who ostensibly conform to the culture's standards of conventional attractiveness and yet who are plagued by feelings of physical inadequacy? You've met them: the size fours who glare at their streamlined thighs and piteously moan about nonexistent saddlebags. If you share my supreme bad judgment, you've probably gone bathing suit shopping with them. We lesser mortals, having spent the better part of the day thinking about, but not using, the *Buns of Steel* exercise video or wondering why our current hair sadist thought Mamie Eisenhower bangs would be a good look, sit mutely by as these more evolved physical specimens discuss with apparently genuine despair their most recently discovered impediment to true beauty. You can tell them they're crazy, but if you're a real friend, you ultimately understand that their anguish, however inexplicable, is real.

My friend Elizabeth is one such woman. Naturally gifted with attributes the cosmetics industry makes a fortune attempting to replicate—large chocolate-brown eyes, a flowing, Pre-Raphaelite mane of hair, the hips of an active adolescent boy—Elizabeth should by all rights be free of the tyranny of physical insecurity. And though a reasonable person in other areas, about her appearance Elizabeth is, in a word, deranged.

Elizabeth happens to be particular about presentation, though she could certainly get away with dressing like a slob. Living with me, she had more than ample opportunity to observe how such laxness might be achieved. But unlike her friend, no dog-chewed bicycle shorts and men's extra-large flannel pajama top would do for Elizabeth. She came into the world with a fully formed sense of style, able to judge instantly whether an article of clothing (often draped over a plastic hanger) would flatter, as well as the good sense to then buy said item (rather than pitch about in a fit of indecision for a week, only to return to find that the item was out of stock). With her unerring fashion sense, Elizabeth is the person we turned to when trying to determine whether platform shoes were just a fad or whether Calvin Klein's knee-length hemline was an act of kindness or misogyny.

Elizabeth and I met nearly fifteen years ago, at a college whose spirit was not unlike a Nazi officer-training camp for preparatory school graduates. This tiny New England idyll, populated by aggressively blond young men and women who seemed to have leapt onto the campus from high-gloss mahogany sailing vessels, was basically what Hitler's fallen army imagined Argentina could be to them. It was not an institution that set much stock in individuality, or even cogent thought, though it was big on fraternal legacy, the androgynous style of dress made popular by J. Crew catalogs, and the social application of Nietzsche's comment: "That which does not destroy me only serves to make me stronger." Suffice it to say, Elizabeth and I became fast, if somewhat desperate, friends.

The defining feature of this academic bastion of privilege was its passionate and defensive love of homogeneity. Before I'd even met her, I'd heard people talk about Elizabeth, who was just then discovering the still-nascent thrift-store chic and oversized silvery jewelry that would in a few years become de rigueur in the vocabulary of hip college outerwear. If it was rankling to listen to comments about the "unusual looking" underclasswoman (she was Italian) who would eventually become one of my closest friends, I was quickly growing accustomed to being rankled in that frantically narrow environment, which was already chafing at me like the control-top pantyhose I struggled into before attending the school's many keg-related formals. What I did not know yet was that the sense of being an outsider, a distinction Elizabeth endured with a graciousness that appeared effortless, was something of which she had had more than her share of experience.

Elizabeth was raised in an academic household. Her father was a distinguished professor of mathematics at one of the nation's most competitive universities, and her mother, after having her children, returned to school for a Ph.D. in chemistry. Elizabeth's older brothers shared, as their singular reason for living, academic excellence and hurtled through college and medical school, coming up for a breath only once their prestigious residencies at top teaching hospitals were ensured. Like many youngest children, Elizabeth was quite gregarious, a quality her family was at a loss to explain. Because she herself was bright and studious, in another family she'd probably have been considered a bit of a straight arrow, but in her own, where the competition was so supremely fierce, her ability to integrate academic and social activities made her a target for the critical wrath of her brothers, who openly dismissed her as a bit of a dilettante.

In time, Elizabeth incorporated her brothers' view of her into her own self-concept—she decided she must be pretty contemptible. Not surprisingly, given her fraternal model for relationships with members of the opposite sex, she tended to be timid and reserved with her male schoolmates. And though she continued to do well in school, she was convinced that this was a result of brute luck. In her heart she knew that to be adequate was all she could hope for, intellectually. By the time she arrived at college, her insecurities were out of control.

One of the first things I noticed about Elizabeth was how dramatically her behavior changed the moment we got involved in any coed situation. On our own, in our dorm rooms or wandering around the campus, she was warm and affectionate, full of easy intimacy or fits of sarcastic, irreverent humor. But the moment one of our male classmates appeared, she would immediately and completely withdraw. At parties or dances, after we had applied coat upon coat of mascara and painstakingly raided each other's closets, Elizabeth presented a surprisingly icy front, a cool disdain bordering on contempt for the very men about whom we had spent hours obsessively talking that very afternoon while lounging on our beds. Even I, who knew her well enough to understand that she was driven by shyness rather than misanthropy, was amazed at the effectiveness of her mask; certainly, any prospective suitors were persuaded that there was no room at Elizabeth's particular inn.

Perplexingly, Elizabeth was as boy-crazy as any of us, spending hours fixated on a look she'd exchanged with a guy in her history class or analyzing a question some fellow had put to her in the lunch line. She recognized that her hostility when she was actually approached in any social setting didn't exactly help in her quest for love. But understand though she did that her behavior was instrumental in her singleness, Elizabeth believed that there was something else standing in her way, and that something was her looks.

Elizabeth was fixated on her appearance, particularly on its horrendous flaws, and she believed it was the albatross she dragged into every social encounter. Of course, her preoccupation with her exterior effectively distracted her from the more worrying inadequacies she'd been persuaded would ultimately be her downfall—those having to do with intelligence, or discipline, or character. And by entering every social situation behind a mask of presumptive hostility, she reinforced her belief that her appearance was ruining every-thing and was able to ignore the fact that it was her own air of negativity, rather than anything to do with the way she looked, that was interfering with her romantic success. As the men around her saw it, Elizabeth was beautiful and cold, which doesn't exactly make for easy access.

Living with Elizabeth, I had ample opportunity to observe her daily routines, and I used to envy the time she took each morning getting dressed. Her complicated and extended clothing ritual sug-gested to me that she anticipated a whole host of extraordinary and pleasant occurrences awaiting her each morning as she left the house. I admit that, on this topic, I was biased. My usual morning routine involved bolting out of bed two minutes before I had to be out of the house, staggering into the bathroom to brush my teeth, and tossing on whatever bedraggled outfit happened to be hanging from the doorknob. I knew that not spending time on how I looked was a form of self-loathing; I did not realize that compulsiveness in the opposite direction might be an expression of the same.

Every morning Elizabeth stood in front of her closet, staring at its contents with a poignant hopefulness that unraveled rapidly into palpable anxiety. She would begin her selection of potential separates—pants and jackets, long skirts, scarves—stepping in and out of them in one well-practiced movement. Do I need to say that any one of the ensembles she was rejecting would have easily earned her a candid photo in the *New York Times* Styles section? Finally, when a mountain of discards lay on the bed, Elizabeth would arrive at the last possible and evidently only acceptable combination, pant-ing from exertion and agitation and spent before the day had even begun.

Once we had graduated and moved to Manhattan, college and its parochial confines happily behind us, Elizabeth's romantic activ-ity—though not necessarily her luck—began to change. Urban men who did not refer to the L.L. Bean catalog as the ideal of female comeliness started flocking around our door. It seemed suddenly that Elizabeth had potential beaux of all sorts from whom to choose. Unfortunately, her romantic life seemed to follow a disturbing pattern. Initially, the men with whom she became involved appeared to appreciate her enormously, paying her compliments and marveling at her many fine qualities. Eventually, though, something would shift, and the warmly affectionate suitor would fade slowly from the picture until, finally, he was gone.

The preoccupation with her appearance and its imaginary problems allowed Elizabeth to remain on fairly superficial terms with her interior self. Naturally, given her estrangement from herself, she could hardly offer much in the way of deep engagement to those men who showed up to take her out for nights on the town. It isn't surprising that most of them gave up in frustration, nor that Elizabeth chose to see their defection as having to do with her lack of physical charm.

Fortunately, something finally broke the spell: Elizabeth decided that she was wasting her time. Whatever obstacles, physical or otherwise, stood in her way, she decided, she might as well figure out what she wanted to do with her life. For all her attention to those obstacles, love or happiness had so far remained elusive; so what did she have to lose?

This was a decision based in pure genius, for it held the power of complete transformation. It was as if Elizabeth's body were a genie bottle and she had decided suddenly to rub her belly, allowing all that had been so long held in to be released. She forced herself to take a hard look at her feelings about her work as a junior investment banker and to accept the fact that she had absolutely no passion for it. Science had always been her real love, specifically veterinary science, but she had suppressed this interest because of the disdain with which her physician brothers had always regarded the discipline, plainly perceiving the care of animals to be the professional equivalent of ladies' room attendant.

Having made the decision to concentrate on her inner rather than exterior self, Elizabeth had little difficulty taking the necessary steps to put her house in order. She abruptly quit her job, in spite of the fact that she had no new job prospects or real sense of what would come next. She spent the next year living very frugally and doing a great deal of thinking. After a brief period of unemployment—including the tremendous first-of-the-month anxiety that only the jobless can truly appreciate—she decided to take a low-level job in a veterinary clinic, determined to see if the reality of working with animals lived up to the fantasy she'd been supressing for so long. She was so relieved when it did that she faced the trauma of applying to veterinary school and the idea of lifelong indenture to the student-loan companies with beatific calm. She entered veterinary school and immediately distinguished herself as a student of extraordinary talent, winning accolades and respect at every turn.

It took Elizabeth awhile to believe in the satisfaction she was experiencing in graduate school, for the respect and admiration she received threatened to subvert a whole lifetime of belief in her own inadequacy. But gradually, over the years, she became more and more comfortable with her success. Engagement with her intellectual and professional life replaced a good deal of the less satisfying attention she'd been paying to romance. And, of course, once she relaxed about her social life, Elizabeth finally met a nice man.

When I was a child, my mother (a woman for whom the desire to have children was tantamount to the desire to live) used to tell me stories about women she knew who had had difficulty conceiving offspring. It seemed that the second these women broke down and adopted babies, they would instantly find themselves pregnant. It was all a question of relaxing, my mother assured me, and despite what I knew about fertility and low sperm count, looking around the neighborhood I could see that there was plenty of flesh-and-blood evidence to back up these stories. It seems that the same theory can be applied to success in romance. But I know there's more to Elizabeth's romantic fulfillment than the fact that she allowed herself to be distracted from her quest. In choosing to devote herself to work that was meaningful and compelling to her, she was not only opening herself up to positive reinforcement and the bolstering of her self-image, she was also allowing herself to develop into a person who had her own interests and goals. It's clear why such a person, in addition to being happier, would be more attractive to others.

Elizabeth now lives with her boyfriend, a man who, in addition to being devoted to her, is genuinely involved in his own intellectual and professional growth. The two seem to have found a fruitful and satisfying balance of togetherness and independence. She continues to struggle with her appearance, though not as compulsively as she once did. Though not behind her, the mornings of trying on every article in her closet are fewer. And while it's clear that she gets plenty of positive reinforcement regarding her looks from her boyfriend, who plainly finds her beautiful, she's also realized that peace with one's physical qualities is not something one finds externally. Just as she has worked so strenuously, and with such superlative results, to overcome her feelings of intellectual undeservedness, so must she continue to confront and challenge those feelings of personal inadequacy that, by attaching themselves to her appearance, have distracted her from the real goal of self-knowledge and acceptance.

I'm not about to pretend that we live in a society that disregards physical appearance, because we definitely do not. But I will say that the amount of importance one decides to imbue one's exterior with is entirely self-regulated. If you make no effort to challenge the idea that your appearance defines and limits you, then by all means it will. And if you decide that there are other far more important things to concentrate on, it will be those considerations that direct the course of your life.

And so, if we rely on the imperfections of our appearance as explanation of or justification for our lack of romantic happiness, we're making a deliberate decision to place great importance on the way we look. And since it's the rare woman who can maintain any semblance of objectivity regarding her appearance, the basis for our insecurities tends to be anything but sound or reasonable anyway.

The chances are good that women who spend an inordinate amount of time worrying about how their looks are affecting their datelessness are using this self-doubt as a way to avoid romantic involvement. Lila and I have done this by colluding with the culture's emphatic preference for Twiggys; Elizabeth has done so by ignoring the fact that she actually does look pretty much the way society wants us to and obsessing anyway.

The impediment to romantic happiness that one's physical characteristics present is entirely self-sustained. In other words, if you have positive feelings about the way you look, people respond in kind. Overattention to one's appearance and its inadequacies is like a giant smokescreen, keeping our attention from the more substantial issue of our interior development and at the same time making it pretty hard to breathe.

8

Portrait of the Artist As a Young Commitment-Phobe

Female Creativity As a Route to Relationship Avoidance

WHEN CONTEMPLATING WOMEN who are reluctant to make a romantic commitment, it's worthwhile to consider what precisely making such a commitment can mean. In the ideal universe, we all easily locate partners who see us clearly and worship us exactly as we are. With this fantasy mate, change or accommodation is so unnecessary as to be anathema. However, the flip side of this fantasy—our very real and often paralyzing fear—is that pledging ourselves to another will mean the exact opposite: the abnegation of our selves, the sublimation of our own identity and needs to another person's or to the union itself.

The women I'll discuss in this chapter have something significant in common: They are artists. Each is serious about and deeply committed to her creative work. I think, not accidentally, each has also had significant difficulty accepting romantic involvement in her life. In fact, only one of these women is actually involved in a relationship, one into which she had to be dragged kicking and screaming, in spite of the fact that she was nuts about the guy.

By the choice of their work, all of these women have indicated that they are capable of commitment—possibly of the most difficult kind, to themselves. And yet their experience suggests that they consider romantic commitment and artistic commitment to be mutually exclusive. So what gives? What does a serious relationship really mean to these women? And what, as they see it, is the price of such a union?

I met Isabel many years ago, in graduate school. She was a student of fine arts, a painter, and known throughout the program as being formidably talented. Her physical appearance recalls an earlier era; were she to slip into something high-necked and brocaded, she would resemble one of those headstrong and radiant women for whom Edith Wharton was forever arranging social calamities. Observing her on campus, I thought she must be the most demure, self-contained person living. Once I got to know her, I found that her cool exterior concealed a raucous, irreverent sense of humor and a villainous wit.

Our friendship had many areas of common ground: We each grew up in large, female-dominated families, we shared a passion in our creative work, and we attempted to restrict our physical activity to only the most crucial tasks, like uncorking bottles of wine or hailing taxicabs. But the surest sign that we would be friends for life was our realization that we shared the distinction of being true girly-girls, a fact that plainly horrified our ultraserious classmates. We regularly escaped the parochial confines of higher study by borrowing a friend's car and racing to the mall, whiling away afternoons trying on high-heeled shoes and lipsticks in deadly shades of red. Our perfect afternoons were those spent lounging on Isabel's couch, wine coolers and Bar-B-Q potato chips by our sides, idly examining that month's *Vogue* and indulging in our favorite topic of conversation: whether the guys we liked liked us.

Men. We were older students, studying the creative arts. Our programs were virtual petri dishes for the ego, especially the male ego. We had our work cut out for us. Remember, in graduate school people are penniless, so these men didn't have access to the usual self-image enhancers such as making a quick half-million in a sexy commodities deal and retiring to the squash court to blow off further competitive steam. And though I have no doubt that the school was filled with well-adjusted potential dates, Isabel and I were extremely adept at locating those who were anything but, those whose greatest pleasure (when they weren't obsessing about their chances for critical acclaim) was toying with our emotions.

Like me, Isabel was no stranger to the allure of attractive, unavailable men. She had a type: dark-haired beauties with sculptured features who radiated intelligence and hinted, with their heavy-lidded eyes, at great cavernous depths. Complicated, mysterious, edgy, these men kept her considerable powers of concentration focused but gave her very little in the way of satisfaction. For what they had in common, besides their rakish good looks, were their withholding natures. Isabel has qualities it would seem impossible not to admire—physical charms, a curious and agile mind, artistic talent, a wicked sense of humor—but these men seemed strangely invulnerable to them. Instead of love or praise or even pleasant companionship, what they offered her was the thrill of the chase, countless hours devoted to intensive behavioral analysis, and, ultimately, lots of solitude.

Just after I met her, Isabel set her cap for a man so inaccessible and remote that years later the mere mention of his name would become a kind of shorthand for our laughably bad romantic judgment. Eli, a sculptor, was just the sort of rumpled genius Isabel couldn't resist—even in this case when there was a very strong hint that perhaps this was an alliance to be avoided. Eli routinely produced sculptures of women that, upon casual perusal, were quite striking and beautiful. Upon closer examination, however (something that the extremely visual Isabel could hardly avoid), it became clear that Eli's clay women were all in some way subtly mutilated:

a missing ear, dents in a breast suggesting previous surgery, too many or few fingers. I don't like to say that the writing was on the wall, but the writing was on the wall.

Unlike me, Isabel doesn't drink three martinis and abandon all thoughts of dignity and the consequences of its absence if she happens to be in the company of a man she likes. Isabel is far more composed in the management of her assignations. She did indulge in the usual subterfuge: arranging to run into him at the student union or art studio, dispatching friends to ascertain his intended whereabouts on a given evening. She did not throw herself at him, for that was decidedly not her style. And for his part, Eli seemed intrigued, if inconsistently so. But he was so plainly absorbed by his own interior clay-related dramas that it was easy to hope that his distractedness around Isabel had more to do with creative epiphanies than romantic ambivalence.

That the chances for this romance's success were slim even I, love's half-wit, could see. Eli was a man capable of devotion, to be sure, and that devotion was, like a boomerang, aimed squarely at himself. Eli was deeply enamored of his own artistic persona. And in case you haven't wasted your youth chasing rock musicians and poets, self-love of this sort doesn't tend to accommodate such unhallowed banalities as dating or boyfriendliness.

All of which Isabel knew. Unfortunately, knowing it did not inspire her to recoil in horror from Eli, as any normal person would. Isabel was far from repelled by the unsavory aspects of her wished-for beau's character; indeed, his self-absorbtion and inscrutability were the very basis for her attraction to him. For a few agonizing months it seemed possible that something would happen—Eli engaged Isabel in brief, intense conversations whenever he happened to run into her, his eyes sought hers at overcrowded parties, he made frequent allusions to various art-related events they might attend together in the future, plans that somehow never seemed to materialize.

And then, devoid of any real climax or explanation, Eli was gone. Well, not gone exactly—he still showed up for classes and openings—just gone from Isabel's area of vision. This was especially disheartening, as Isabel could hardly call him and demand an explanation. "Why have you ended our non-relationship?" doesn't exactly translate into a winning premise for a casual conversation. Which is not to say that Isabel briskly cut her losses and moved on. Eli's defection provided material for at least a year of anguished analysis. Rare Eli sightings could fuel an entire week of rumination. Isabel knew that she was encroaching on lunatic territory, but it was a long time before the hold Eli and his detachment carnival had on her tenacious heart eased.

From the time that she was a child, Isabel has had a serious interest in art. Her identification of herself as a painter has been the defining constant of her life, in spite of the usual self-doubt and bouts of unproductiveness. Whether enrolled in an academic program or simply working on her own, Isabel has struggled to paint even during those times when she's had virtually no feedback or reinforcement. She has deliberately arranged her life so that she has both the abundant time and solitude her work requires. Her commitment to her work is as much a part of her life as breathing or coffee, essential and immutable. She's not especially interested in the outer trappings of artistic life; she just wants to paint.

Because I was engaged just as strenuously in my own relationship avoidance during the period I've described, I was not inclined to consider the implications of Isabel's romantic choices. I did not see that her attraction to men who would not deign to become involved with her had much to do with her fear of what she might have to sacrifice to a serious relationship. Neither did I recognize that Isabel, drawn to men who would refuse involvement, herself feared that such involvement would threaten the privacy and fecund fantasy life that she believed made her creative work possible. I just thought she liked mean guys.

Once her program was completed, Isabel was offered a position at the university teaching art classes. She accepted the job in large part because she knew it would allow her sufficient time to concentrate on her own painting. Shortly after taking the job, she renewed her friendship with another painter, Andrew, a man she'd known casually in the past but with whom she'd lost contact.

That Andrew had romantic feelings for her was soon apparent to everyone but Isabel. She allowed that he seemed to enjoy spending time with her and that they shared a whole host of similar interests, from Francis Bacon to O. J. Simpson, but insisted that Andrew desired only a platonic friendship with her. He was an extremely attractive man who'd had a number of apparently serious girlfriends, and Isabel seemed to find it impossible to fathom that he might be genuinely interested in her.

Isabel's deliberate denseness in response to the clear signals Andrew was putting out served her by keeping him at bay for a while. When someone repeatedly deflects your attempts at greater intimacy, it's easy to believe that person is simply not interested. Fortunately, Andrew was not prepared to give up without a fight— he was crazy about Isabel and was determined not to let her squirm away. As he grew more ardent in his attempts to get involved, Isabel began to panic. Before Andrew's interest in her became too obvious to deny, she had harbored her usual silent crush on him. However, once it was undeniable, even to her, that he returned her romantic feelings, she was suddenly overcome by doubt.

She called me one night in the midst of all of this, her voice full of dread. "What am I doing?" she whispered. "I must be crazy. We should just stay friends, because I know this isn't going to work out." In all the years I'd known her, I'd never heard Isabel sound so frightened. And even though I'd not yet met Andrew, I sensed that she was not so much afraid their relationship would fail but that it would succeed. It was obvious that she felt cornered, trapped in a situation that had real power to harm her. Andrew, it seemed, was interested in more than Isabel's usual objectification festival; he wanted to have an actual relationship. *With her.*

It's lucky that Andrew was patient and that he was certain about his feelings, for Isabel was not easily persuaded. Even after they got together, the first several months of their relationship were marked by progress and setbacks, the latter mostly in the form of her nervous ambivalence about the intimacy between them. It took a long time for her to believe that Andrew could accept her as she was, and that while he did require her to participate in the relationship and to be attentive to him, as he was to her, he did not want her to abandon the person she was or the work she did. As a painter himself, Andrew understood completely what it meant to care deeply about one's work and to be protective about the rituals needed to do it. It was a long time before Isabel could admit, even to herself, that she was genuinely in love with Andrew. "I kept fighting it," she admits now, laughing at herself. "I convinced myself that I could back out at any time. Until, finally, I realized that I just didn't want to."

Isabel can see now that, however miserable she believed herself to be at the time, the Elis of her past served her purposes pretty well. "Those relationships, for lack of a better word, took place entirely in my head. So I was completely in control. I never had to deal with interference from the other person or even think of him, except in the ways that suited my mood at the moment." This arrangement also served her, as it did not challenge her various eccentricities, in particular her worrying tendency toward reclusiveness. On some level, Isabel must have feared that the other sort of relationship, the kind in which one actually has to participate, would undermine her commitment to her work. And as her work was such an essential aspect of her identity, this was not a risk she'd been willing to take.

For most of her life she'd seen herself as someone who was thwarted and had suffered in love. She believed, in accordance with the Romantic view of art, that this suffering was the wellspring for her creative productivity. (Many youngsters are partial to this theory. Later on, with the passage of time and the loss of one's epidermal elasticity, one begins to understand that a wallet full of functioning credit cards and the presence of a dutiful au pair are the true requirements for a successful artistic life. But I digress.)

Though she would have denied it during her great Eli vigil, Isabel believed on some level that the pain and alienation she endured in the name of love both suffused her paintings with intensity and passion and ensured her the solitude she imagined she needed to focus her work. It's no wonder that the prospect of pairing up with Andrew filled her with worry; it must have seemed to her that she was being forced to make a choice between love and, as Wordsworth described it, "that inward eye which is the bliss of solitude." Or, more bluntly, she must have felt as if she were choosing between Andrew and herself.

This conundrum ultimately sorted itself out very happily, in large part because Isabel eventually decided to come to her senses. She took several thousand deep breaths and, concluding that her feelings for Andrew were too powerful to abandon, she took the plunge. And in the years that they've been together, Isabel has indeed changed, though not in ways she could have anticipated.

As her relationship with Andrew has shifted from agitated infatuation into a supportive and loving partnership, Isabel has had far more energy for her painting. In the absence of the elaborate distraction of trying to please a difficult potential boyfriend, her concentration is better, her focus clearer. Not only is she considerably more prolific than in the past, but her work has taken entirely new and original directions as she has found herself released from her previous state of constant frustration and emotional chaos. She was recently invited to participate in a group show at a prominent New York art gallery, an invitation that carries the attendant possibility of representation by said gallery. All because she finally lowered the drawbridge and offered entry to the world.

Isabel fought love, but it managed to force its way into her life almost in spite of her. Karen, on the other hand, is fighting love and winning. Karen is a playwright whom I met a few years ago when she moved to my neighborhood in lower Manhattan to oversee the Off-Off-Broadway production of a play she'd written. Like Isabel, Karen is passionately committed to her creative life. After years of struggle and relative isolation eking out a living in smaller, cheaper cities, she has finally begun to receive the critical attention and praise she deserves. In the last few years, she's been awarded several prestigious playwriting grants, and, after the success of her first, a second play is now in the early stages of production.

No one is more aware than Karen of the sacrifices and delayed gratification involved in this lengthy enterprise—the roach-infested apartments, the pecuniary magic acts demanded by any unexpected expense, the spirit-leeching rigors of public transportation—and she approaches the successes she's had so far with a kind of guarded euphoria. She's both excited and grateful, and she wants to do everything she can to ensure that this taste of success snowballs into something on the order of the spread in *Babette's Feast.*

Given the frequency with which the subject of romance turns up in her plays, most viewers tend to assume that Karen must be the Aphrodite of theater, a seasoned veteran of love's battles. And while her observations on the subject are perceptive and sophisticated, the fact is that it's been years since her last relationship.

Believe me when I superficially assure you that Karen is a very attractive woman. Tall, curvaceous, the sort of sweet face magazine editors persist in describing as heart-shaped, and the smooth complexion possessed by certain black women who will continue to be mistaken for college students long after they've become grandmothers. Furthermore, she's willing to put some effort into her appearance, tearing herself out of bed every morning at six and suiting up for a lengthy run that does God knows what damage to the irreplaceable cartilage in her knees. Consequently, she has one of those rippling, "cut" bodies one normally only finds in swimsuit calendars or on the girlfriends of rock stars. When her run is completed, she remembers to stretch (a critical ritual some of us habitually overlook, only to awaken the next day to find that our legs have petrified like trees); after a brisk shower, she settles in at her desk, ready to write. It's appalling.

Men are attracted to Karen not just because the flesh on her upper arms is dimple-free but because of the quality of attention she brings to her interactions with them. When you talk to her, she listens, digesting what you've said before responding with intelligence and care. And frankly, the acclaim she's received in the last few years hasn't hurt in terms of meeting interesting single men. But in spite of the numerous invitations and compliments, Karen remains unattached. She bemoans her lack of a love life and claims that she really wants to get involved in a relationship. But something is clearly holding her back.

Karen's most serious relationship to date ended about three years ago. She'd lived with Tom, her boyfriend, for almost four years, and although it was she who finally called it quits, it's obvious that she remains confused about him. According to Karen, Tom was drop-dead handsome, extremely creative, and possessed of a sexual charisma that she, during their extended courtship, found impossible to resist.

Karen met Tom, a marginally talented actor, when he landed a small role in a play of hers being performed at a regional theater in the midwestern city where she then lived. The chemistry between them was so powerful that, despite her awareness of his reputation as a ladykiller, she could not resist his overtures.

An affair ensued, one lent an impressive degree of passionate drama by Tom's ever-changing level of involvement. If one day she was the love of his life, the next he'd decide that the entire concept of monogamy was barbaric, and the day after that announce he'd made a terrible mistake and beg for her forgiveness. This roller-coaster ride was punctuated by bouts of incredible physical passion, which Karen even then recognized were heightened by the hovering threat of another reversal. Tom's indecisive heart caused her enormous anguish, but her unhappiness was tempered by the fact that in their better moments, she felt that he was perfect for her—he shared her passion for the theater as well as a similar aesthetic sensibility, and physically he was irresistible.

When, early into their fourth year together, Karen was offered a fellowship that included a year of travel, she was forced to make a decision. She knew that her relationship with Tom could go on indefinitely. She also believed that the amount of time and energy she spent each day obsessing about the ultimate direction of his feelings was interfering with her ability to focus on her work. So strong were her feelings for Tom that she imagined the separation might kill her, but the alternative of ongoing uncertainty had begun to seem like a comparably dismal option. She accepted the fellowship.

Karen did survive the separation and, professionally at least, has thrived. In the years since she broke off with Tom, her writing has matured significantly. Her newer plays explore an increasingly raw and brutal level of emotion and are distinguished by a structural complexity and assurance that sometimes startles critics. Even Karen can't deny that her work has improved.

Recently, I arranged to meet Karen for a drink after seeing a preview performance of her latest play. I admit I hadn't been entirely prepared for the performance, which initially seemed to chronicle the experiences of a woman who fearfully suspects that her grown son is a chronic rapist and concludes by demonstrating the almost shocking level of collusion between mother and son. After somewhat breathlessly congratulating Karen, I decided to ask her if there'd been some identifiable turning point in her work.

"Sure," she responded ruefully. "Everything changed when I gave up men."

When I asked her to explain, Karen paused briefly before answering. "When I was with Tom, I spent a disgusting amount of time trying to keep the whole thing together. Either I'd be anticipating his moods, or trying to stave them off, or giving in to them. And every time he called things off, got cold feet or whatever, I'd be so destroyed I'd just get in bed and sleep for three days." She shook her head in something like disbelief. "So you can imagine how much time I spent writing. I think in the four years, I managed to get maybe half a play written."

"And you found you could work once you were on your own?"

"Well, not at first. The fellowship year was a total waste. I spent six months in Paris sitting on the floor of my hotel room eating bonbons. But once I got back home—Tom moved out after we broke up—I was able to settle in and work. I'd spent so much time alone in Europe that I guess I just got used to it. And something was changing in my writing; that was obvious. I was beginning to go much deeper."

Karen sipped her drink and looked pensive. "It was really good for me to get out on my own. It released me, somehow, creatively. I wasn't trying to be anything for anyone, so I was free to sort of think about whatever I liked. Which was incredibly liberating."

"So, what about now? Would you even want to be in a relationship at this point?"

"I do," Karen said quickly. "Very much. I spend a lot of time thinking about it, worrying that time is passing and if I'm going to try to make a life with someone, the time to do it is now. It's just that after all this time on my own, I can't see getting involved with anyone who didn't make my life better than it already is. Someone who wasn't supportive and whose own life wasn't already in pretty good shape.

"But there's another part of me, the bad part, that feels like that kind of relationship would be so boring. So predictable. I think

I'd miss the excitement and just lose interest. So I don't know. I'm sort of stuck."

Karen's fear is a complicated one, complicated because it's also a desire—a paradox Alfred Hitchcock made famous in *Vertigo*. The consuming intensity of her relationship with Tom not only interfered with her ability to work—or for that matter to remember to leave the house or feed herself—but also was thrilling and perilous. When the powerful affections of your beloved seem as easy to turn on and off as a household appliance, you exchange stability for the titillation of high drama. And drama, however exhausting and infuriating, also tends to be fairly addictive. Karen's relationship with Tom convinced her that real love involves manipulation and uncertainty, elements that her increased self-awareness rejects. But on the other hand, she is both doubtful that romantic involvement can be a nurturing experience and concerned that, even if it could be, her own attraction to high romantic drama might render her an unsuitable candidate for this healthier sort of coupling.

Karen feels pretty acutely the absence of a partner in her life. It's been a long time since she had someone to send out in the middle of the night to buy ice cream, or holler for when she spied a waterbug, or go to bed with. She's not quite at the point where she can accept that the theatrics to which she is so drawn are now exactly where they should be: on the stage. Nor does she see that were another high-maintenance romance like the one she had with Tom to come her way, she'd last about a week before shaking her head in impatience and packing her bags.

Karen's next move—the one that will lead her to a new level of romantic engagement—is going to require a certain leap of faith. Her inability to make that leap, to let her guard down and trust that relationships can improve, rather than detract from, one's life, assures her single status. But it's a leap she will make, for the intimate relationship she's been able to establish with herself will guide her in the right direction emotionally, just as it has with her creative work.

In the battle between love and work, work is the clear victor in Jane's life. Unlike Isabel and Karen, Jane has had very limited experience with men, and at first glance it appears that she's arranged her life very nicely without the benefit of a partner. She makes a fairly good living as a freelance editor and has considerable time left over to concentrate on her first love, writing poetry. Over the years, her poems have appeared in increasingly prestigious publications, and she recently experienced that nonpareil of poetry triumphs: publication in *The New Yorker*. Her first collection of poems is nearing completion, and a few of the magazine editors she's worked with over the years have offered to help her place it with a publishing house when she's ready.

Jane grew up in Massachusetts as the third daughter born to an old and distinguished Boston Brahmin family. She was raised amid the comfort and privilege of Beacon Hill by parents whose jaws mysteriously tightened whenever they spoke. Jane's mother and father employed scads of household help and vacationed frequently, instructing Jane to press the small bell beside her bed whenever she wished to summon her nanny. Even as a small child, she found the rigid conservatism of her parents' home stifling and invited their disapproval by seeking out friends she remembers her parents describing more than once as "riffraff."

Jane attended college in Chicago, a decision that dismayed practically everyone, especially given the close proximity to her home of both Mount Holyoke and Wellesley. And after graduating, she simply stayed, refusing her family's repeated efforts to bribe her into returning. She spent several years living in downtown Chicago before deciding to buy a charming if somewhat ramshackle farmhouse about an hour north of the city. Not accidentally, Jane's best friend, Carol, owns a house about five miles away from Jane's.

Jane and Carol met in college and became close immediately. Jane, in spite of having distanced herself physically from her roots, retains a certain cool reserve; one can actually sense the pause before she allows herself to react. Carol, on the other hand, is a creature of impulse, exuberant and emotional and utterly unable to censor herself. While at school, Jane spent most nights squirreled away in the dorm room the two shared, reading Milton and Dryden and earnestly attempting to puzzle out the structural mysteries of the sestina (an exercise in futility, in case you've never tried). Carol, on the other hand, preferred to pass most evenings on an extended tour of the city's gin mills and jazz clubs, rarely stumbling home before dawn.

After college, Carol found a job in her field of study—social work—while Jane started slowly taking on freelance editing jobs. The two continued to live together, and, just as in college, Jane tended to shy away from social life. Although Jane, with her well-made features and the sort of enviable figure that is the genetic reward for hundreds of years spent horseback riding, was on paper probably the more attractive of the two, Carol was the one men pursued. Though Jane admits that it was sometimes difficult to watch Carol getting ready night after night, fixing her makeup or spritzing perfume or trying to locate just one pair of still-decent pantyhose, she also insists that Carol's regular absence from their apartment gave Jane plenty of time to concentrate on her poetry.

"If Carol had been less gregarious, I probably wouldn't have gotten anything done. On the nights she was home, I always managed to abandon everything and watch movies with her. We'd lay on the couch like two beached whales, with giants bags of Cool Ranch Doritos on our laps. Carol was always giving herself a pedicure, and usually she'd convince me that I needed one, too. It was impossible to get work done when she was around."

Shortly after Carol accepted a new job as a social worker at a local hospital, she met Gary, a pediatric resident. After just a few dates, Carol announced that she was wildly in love and could barely stand to wait until Gary proposed marriage. As it turned out, she didn't have to wait long: less than three months later they were engaged.

Jane was thrilled for her friend and joined her in planning the elaborate nuptials Carol had long envisioned. She accompanied Carol on expeditions to bridal shops to search for a gown, to potential reception sites, to photographers and florists. She counseled Carol during her inevitable preceremony disagreements with her fiancé and, on not a few occasions, offered Gary a shoulder to cry on as well. When I asked her if she didn't feel a bit envious of all this activity, she said no.

"I guess in a funny way I felt it was my wedding, too. I was so involved with every decision and really excited about it. Also, Gary was different than most of Carol's other boyfriends, in that he seemed to really want a friendship with me. In the past, guys would show up to collect Carol and act like I was some piece of furniture they had to step around. Gary would sit and talk or ask if I wanted to join them. Sometimes the three of us just hung out together at home. It was really nice."

Carol moved out of her apartment with Jane and into Gary's. Carol's new place was only about eight blocks from the apartment she and Jane used to share, and the three friends continued to spend a great deal of time together. Eventually, though, Carol and Gary decided to start looking for a house to buy. As Gary had grown up in the country, the couple started exploring a rural area north of Chicago. After a few months of searching, they found what they felt was the perfect house.

It was only when Jane learned that Carol and Gary would be moving farther away than walking distance that the real impact of Carol's marriage hit her. For years, in spite of Carol's countless relationships, Jane had felt that the two of them were a team. And even after the wedding, it was as if Gary had simply become part of that team. The idea that they could just up and move away, leaving her to fend for herself, made Jane lightheaded with panic. Feeling abandoned, Jane forced herself to concentrate on her writing, working late into the night. It was only when poised intently before her typewriter that she could forget the fact that, for the first time in years, she was genuinely alone.

Although she lived only a short plane ride away from Boston (not that any plane ride seems short to a person such as myself, who has been known to shriek, "We're going to crash!" during perfectly routine landings), Jane's visits home were infrequent and brief. She especially loved her mother, but it was difficult for Jane to spend much time with her. To Jane her mother seemed lost, so completely unable to assert herself that she seemed to have virtually no opinions or attitudes. It was clear to Jane that this enforced neutrality was the result of mother's efforts during the entire course of her marriage to please her difficult and demanding husband.

Jane has vague memories of her mother when she was young, teasing her children, teaching them the lyrics to her favorite songs, climbing down onto the floor to play with them. She also remembers, not so vaguely, the fury this behavior would inspire in Jane's father, who had very particular ideas about how a proper wife should behave. Through the course of the marriage Jane watched her mother gradually abandon many things—her career, her friendships and interests outside the home, and finally a substantial part of her personality—all in the interest of marital accord. Given the example before her, it's little wonder Jane did everything in her power to avoid even the most casual contact with men.

Jane identified so strongly with her mother that she felt each criticism and restriction leveled by her father as if it were directed at her. As a result of this, she was a pretty miserable child. It was only when she began reading poetry, and eventually writing it, that she began to experience a kind of freedom from the tyranny of her father's control. To Jane the ability to explore her imagination, to experience autonomous ideas and emotions, was as exhilarating as extreme skiing or skydiving might be to someone else. And even as an adult, she remained so protective of her writing and the independent identity it represented that she felt she couldn't risk attempting to get close to anyone who might ultimately want her to stop being herself.

Which is not to say she happily accepted her self-enforced solitude. Her dependence on Carol and the more full life she's been able to make is a fairly clear indication of that. Not six months after Carol and Gary bought their new house, Jane decided to purchase a house for herself in the area. And when Carol had her first, then second baby, Jane became like a second mother to the children, lavishing them with attention and care. And while this arrangement may sound odd (sort of like the makings of a sequel to *The Hand That Rocks the Cradle*), the fact is that Carol and Gary are overjoyed by Jane's presence in their lives. They simply see her as one of the family.

For Jane, however, the situation is somewhat less than ideal. She's so involved with Carol and Gary's family because she herself so badly wants one and because this is as close as she can let herself get. She says about her friends, "I look at them sometimes, Carol and Gary, and I wonder if behind all their joviality there's some dark side. Some control he has over her that I just can't see." It's clear from this comment that Jane continues to believe that an intimate relationship must extract a high price from its participants. The commitment she's made to her poetry is a commitment to the perservation of her own identity. Unfortunately, it is this identity that she believes is the currency with which one buys one's way into a relationship. By observing the union between Carol and Gary, she can see that this needn't necessarily be the case. But she won't entirely dispel this fear until she decides to become available to closeness with another person, opening herself up to experiences of her own.

In in a world that often seems to undervalue artists, making and sustaining a commitment to one's creative work can be a serious challenge. Obviously, this commitment can be made easier by certain factors in one's life. Enough free time to have an occasional cogent thought is useful, as is having sufficient money to buy groceries. Neighbors who refrain from playing salsa music until dawn are good, and so are art or office-supply stores willing to run a tab. For a young artist, any of the above elements can mean the difference between the happy completion of a project and the failure of same. And as such failure can bring about the decidedly unhappy response of banging one's head against the floor until one suffers brain-stem injury, most people engaged in creative work would probably agree that these little things really do mean a lot.

And yet when it comes to the one factor that really makes life easier—the presence of a supportive, loving partner—many female artists react to this possibility as if it were an invitation to shove their fists into a whirring garbage disposal. They believe (sometimes consciously, as in the case of Isabel and Karen; sometimes not, as with Jane) that intimacy with a partner will significantly compromise their creative work. And yet, the frustration and conflict that can arise as one attempts to deflect intimate engagement can create far more serious impediments to creativity.

Of course, this theory that the presence of a good-hearted partner lessens the burden of daily toil and actually increases one's chances for success has a broader application than the creative arena alone. One needn't be painting the Sistine Chapel to benefit from a healthy romantic union. As Isabel's experience suggests, involvement in a secure relationship, and the ensuing abatement of romantic anxiety, can actually free one to focus more productively and with greater satisfaction on one's goals, whatever they may be.

9

Free Birds

Commitment Anxiety and
the Dream of the Remade Self

COMMITTING TO A RELATIONSHIP is serious business, for the decision to join romantic forces is one that reverberates through all areas of our lives. When we throw open the doors of our hearts to another, we're agreeing to more than the complete refurbishing of our beau's wardrobe or the cultivation of a concerned expression whenever the phrase *baseball strike* is used in conversation. Implicit in the whole notion of commitment is the willingness to allow another person access to our private, well-kept, secret self. This can be a tremendously intimidating proposition, for it requires that we bare to our beloved not only the kicky stewardess who mixes excellent drinks and keeps her roots touched up, but that other person as well, that not very nice girl to whom the PMS defense in murder trials has a very satisfying, and really quite personal, appeal. The decision to let ourselves be fully known by the person we care about carries with it the understanding that, once we've allowed our whole selves to be seen, our partner will be compelled to make a judgment concerning his or her desire to accept or reject the true, unreconstituted, and sometimes not very well behaved reality of who we actually are.

Generally speaking, this exercise in romantic full disclosure carries the attendant hope that once we've let our too-often-unwashed hair down, our lovers will embrace us in our imperfect entirety, whereupon the experience of true and affirming acceptance will be ours; certainly this is the reigning wisdom of the greeting card industry. At which point, the creepshow of insecurity and despair huddling just below the surface of our rigidly cheerful exterior will, under the unconditionally loving gaze of our partner, be forever exiled, or at least put into reasonably manageable perspective.

For obvious reasons, the bleak alternative to this scenario—being booted out the door without a fare-thee-well or backward glance—can act as a powerful inhibitor to our desire for such intimacy. Ours is the culture responsible for the creation of feminine hygiene spray; why should we have any confidence that when the time comes to remove our control-top pantyhose (proving to our boyfriends that the term *paunch* knows no gender boundaries) or admit that we can't remember who the secretary of state is, the phone won't instantly fall silent and the love of our life go permanently AWOL?

The possibility that once you share your private vulnerabilities and quirks with your beloved he'll turn on you like a foam-mouthed dog can be reason enough to keep a lid on the impulse toward full disclosure. However, there are certain women to whom the prospect of rejection, grim though it might be to the rest of us, is as nothing compared to the true and enduring terror that keeps them, like sharks, perpetually on the move. Unlike the female artists in the preceding chapter who worry that romantic engagement will replace their ability to do their creative work, these women are terrified that the moment they break down and commit to another person, they'll plunge into a deep freeze, permanently halted in their own internal development, deprived of new experience, all their fine potential lost. I'm not kidding. They're nuts.

Which is not to say that these women don't have relationships.

They're forever hurling themselves into passionate unions, convinced that they've achieved nirvana, that they've finally found Mr. Right. But you can count on the fact that, sooner or later, regardless of how genuinely wonderful their current man might be, these women will start itching to get free. They begin to feel constricted or trapped, start compulsively listing their boyfriends' faults, daydream fanatically about other, more "appropriate" or "interesting" romantic possibilities. To these women, commitment means entrapment, a diminishment of their own selves. It doesn't really matter whether they're dating Denzel Washington or Steve Urkel, the truth is that when the time comes to get serious, what these women get is panicked.

What is it about seeing someone's toothbrush hanging in their bathroom that makes these women grow prostrate with anxiety? Why does the receipt of a girlfriend's wedding invitation foster fantasies of leaping up to object during the ceremony? Why does communion with another soul feel to them not like an expansion, a blossoming, but rather certain and ineluctable death?

I met Kate in graduate school where, unlike me, she was busily preparing for a profession in a lucrative field: the law. She rented an apartment in a house down the block from mine in the snowy upstate New York valley where we then lived, and I would often see her stomping out in her red scarf and mittens to clear off the foot or so of snow that accumulated every night on our sidewalks. My roomates and I did not own a shovel, though we would on occasion concede to the inclemency of the region by tossing a desultory handful of salt toward the front steps and blithely hoping for the best. I remember sitting perched in my window seat as the winter sun began to set, drinking Tab, smoking cigarettes, and wondering where in the world Kate got her formidable energy.

As I began to get to know her, it became clear that her discipline and will were not limited to her domestic chores. Kate was at that time a second-year law student who divided her time winningly between managing grueling course work, editing the law review, and holding down two jobs to pay her living expenses. In the hope that she would secure a decently paying job upon emerging with her degree, Kate had fearlessly accepted the usual gargantuan student loans necessary to meet the university's tuition. Every month when the time came to write out rent checks or pay the heating company, her anguish would be almost palpable as she tried to piece together the means to keep her meager lifestyle afloat. And yet in spite of the financial anxiety, her dedication to her academic duties never foundered. I was bent rather aggressively on the avoidance of work, then as now, and often interrupted her studying with the suggestion that we go shoe shopping or watch *Terms of Endearment* on video again, but Kate was wise to my ploys and always firmly declined. Though she was enormously amusing company during her free time, she would not be distracted from her more serious commitments.

That Kate did not have a great deal of extra time to devote to social life was not an altogether bad thing, considering the type of men to whom she was attracted. The law school was filled with tort-obsessed megalomaniacs who lulled themselves to sleep each night with visions of Supreme Court appointments and who clearly felt a seething resentment toward their female classmates and the appalling competition they represented. Never one to shy away from a challenge, Kate invariably chose the most offensive of these prospects, the most alcoholic and misogynistic specimen, upon whom to lavish her considerable devotion. It is not an exaggeration to say that the more badly behaved a particular fellow, the more intriguing he would seem to Kate. If pressed, she would describe her current crush as "spirited" or "lively." "Guys who are overly available bore me," she'd say, yawning with affected ennui, pretending not to be monitoring the entrance of whichever bar we happened to be sitting in to see if her crush du jour would deign to make an appearance. Raising her eyebrows in mock disdain, she'd drawl, "Where's the challenge?"

Luckily for her, most of the relationships Kate coveted remained purely hypothetical, as the men she liked tended to be adamantly opposed to any kind of substantial involvement. They were not, however, loath to engage in the occasional amorous tête-à-tête, especially after an evening of steady drinking. She had a hard time accepting the fact that a man's willingness to spend the night with her did not automatically translate into the desire to, say, stay for breakfast. No matter how many times she was misled by a suitor's gin-soaked conviviality, she seemed incapable of learning from experience. This particular inability led to a considerable amount of misery for Kate, for her friends, and probably for the hungover guys skulking out her back door at six A.M.

So when Kate finally met Nick, a man willing to stick around for waffles after a roll in the hay, her other friends and I breathed a collective sigh of relief. A year behind Kate academically, Nick was evidently grateful to have a more seasoned companion to show him the ropes, help edit his papers, sooth his frazzled nerves. And Kate, overburdened though she was, seemed happy to comply. She threw herself into domestic contentedness—not difficult, as Nick virtually moved in with her after their first date—and it was weeks before any of us managed to clap eyes on her.

When she finally broke down and decided to throw a little dinner party to present her new beau, the news was met with some excitement. I decided to arrive a bit early on the appointed evening, intending to lend her a hand with her dinner preparations. I confess I hoped to have a moment or two to converse with Kate's suitor, something that proved impossible, given his unwillingness to wrest himself from the television set, on which a playoff game was being aired. I hovered in the kitchen as Kate fussed with napkins and silverware, stealing furtive glances toward the next room where Nick, bathed in ghostly television light and sipping a beer, made appreciative sports-fan noises.

The situation didn't improve with the arrival of Kate's other guests. We stood in the kitchen, drinking wine, while Kate put dinner on the table. Nick waited until the last possible moment to slip into his seat, one eye cocked surreptitiously toward the television, its volume turned low. He wolfed his meal between long draughts of beer, grunting in response to the group's efforts to include him in conversation and then quickly excused himself from the table. We bid Kate farewell to the sound of Nick's frenzied cry, "It's good!"

Okay, so he was obviously a loser. Obvious to us, perhaps, but evidently not to Kate, who, rather than listen to her friends grumble about her new beau's bad behavior, began to keep a very low profile. Of course, now that she was cohabiting with Nick, she didn't have a copious amount of time for socializing anyway, what with all the hours she had to put in typing her beloved's papers and keeping him in clean socks. Supplication usually requires a time commitment, and Kate was never one to shirk from her self-imposed duties.

Though Kate rarely had the means to feed herself decently, her involvement with Nick signaled the end of pecuniary moderation. She went into debt stocking the house with the imported beer and cuts of sirloin Nick required to get through a tough night of study. Where the old Kate had forced herself to live with the heat turned down to 60, the new one's concern about Nick's gentleflower susceptibility to the elements cranked the furnace up to full tilt. Needless to say, Nick was disinclined to contribute financially to this cozy domestic arrangement—not that Kate pushed, mind you—as doing so smelled suspiciously of serious commitment to him, a responsibility for which (despite the stacks of freshly laundered clothing lining his drawers) he was decidedly not in the market.

Despite the obvious disadvantages of sharing one's home with emotional roadkill, Kate gave all signs of appreciating the benefits of full-time love. She did, after all, have a boyfriend now—someone to sit on the couch and study with, someone to wake up with on those snowy mornings when the thought of climbing out from under the covers is beyond endurance. And though Nick sometimes behaved devilishly, he was merely doing what a user does, which is use. Far more mysterious was Kate's attraction (apart from the obvious availability of a hand to hold during scary movies) to the presence of a partner who made her already difficult life considerably harder and whose pupils seemed unable to focus on her unless she was standing before him with a heaping plate of food.

To the uninitiated, the innocent, Kate would probably appear to be the quintessential Dirt Girl, gripped with self-loathing and doubt, desperate for male attention in any form, no matter how flawed. However, one should not be satisfied with such easy explanations, especially if one has tuned into *The X Files*, thus learning a thing or two about the frequency with which things are more complicated than they seem. Those of us who have accepted as our mantle, our mission, the subversion of conventional analysis, to whom the phrase *grassy knoll* cannot be slipped into conversation often enough, are not satisfied with Quick-Draw McGraw explanations. We're truth hunters, and we want some answers. Right?

Our first clue that Kate was playing a game of her own devising cropped up a few months into her liaison with Nick. While he had evidently appreciated having the Saint Pauli Girl at his beck and call for the initial period of their time together, eventually he began to become frustrated by Kate's implacability. It seemed that his feelings for her were deepening, she reported one afternoon when she'd sought refuge and a cup of coffee at my apartment. He wanted the two of them to be closer. He was—*gasp*—falling in love with her. Kate related this information as though she were describing a band of blood-sucking leeches that had somehow managed to attach themselves to her leg. And it wasn't too long after that visit that the neighborhood was privy to the spectacle of Nick's belongings being piled onto the sidewalk, awaiting collection by their newly independent owner.

Kate rarely carped about having to drag herself up at the crack of dawn to her various part-time jobs serving breakfast to or facilitating the library needs of pearl-adorned undergraduates, so it would have been easy to assume that she was simply blessed with the jolly-slave constitution that makes such hardship bearable. She certainly played the part well, a regular Ben Franklin in her portrayal of work ethic in action. One had to look pretty closely to notice the small grimace lines on her forehead or the tense set of her jaw as she prepared to leave for yet another task, suggesting that the kingdom was not quite as peaceable as it seemed. Beneath her tidily pleasant exterior beat the heart of a seditionist. She was not cheerful, she was determined, and there's a world of difference between the two. Her discretion functioned as the metaphorical finger in the dike, the slightest movement of which would bring forth a cascade of something she badly wanted to contain.

The better I got to know Kate, the more certain details from her past perplexed me. For someone whose kitchen cabinets generally contained two boxes of generic macaroni and cheese and who sucked ice cubes between meals, she seemed to have had a curiously exotic childhood. There we'd be, curled up on the couch watching some PBS program on Gertrude Stein, and Kate would point to a charming limestone building on the same block and mention that she'd spent a summer living in that house when she was nine. Or I'd persuade her to join me for a complicated Thai dinner, one for whose preparation I'd happily squandered my study hours, and while we were eating she'd share a memory of having gotten terribly sick during a visit to Bangkok.

Kate had attended a very exclusive and prohibitively costly preparatory school, and there was nothing she enjoyed more than reminiscing about the time she spent there, riding horses and reading Greek. It was difficult to reconcile those tales of aristocracy with her current Dickensian existence, and one night when she was wringing her hands about the electricity being shut off once again, I broke down and asked her if maybe her parents couldn't loan her a bit of money to tide her over.

"Are you insane?" was her reply. "They can't even make their mortgage payments. They'll probably be moving in with me soon." Her voice was bitter as she proceeded to pour out the sad tale of her family's fall from financial grace. Kate, it seemed, had been born into a family of serious wealth, generations upon generations of dividend checks, and during the course of her short life she had watched the money, all the beautiful money, simply disappear. Her father had taken it upon himself to tackle the stock market, and the market had won.

The rags-to-riches shift in Kate's lifestyle was dramatic. As her father began his first job hunt, she cut up her I. Magnin charge card and attempted to comprehend the fact that her future was to be dramatically different than she'd once imagined. Tossed out were her applications to Harvard and Yale, her precollege European tour, the black convertible MG she'd had her eye on. Gone as well were the assumptions of privilege and ascension that had been an integral part of her identity since birth.

Kate had been raised as a part of the ruling class, and her distinction as such was not something she relinquished willingly. The indignities she had had to suffer since her family's plunge into poverty were truly that: a bad dream from which she was determined to eventually awaken. The poor Kate was not resigned to her fate; she was rigidly biding her time until real life resumed and in the meantime enduring her necessary impostor's role of pauper.

So, you're wondering, what does this have to do with Nick or any of the other potential beaux with whom she had the misfortune to butt heads during our academic adventures? More than you might think. Kate had made the unendurable endurable by creating a sharp division in herself—the public Kate, who traveled amiably to the mall to seek employment at the local Orange Julius, and the private one, who believed that she would one day vindicate her personal setbacks by striding into a courtroom and coolly arguing a case before an appropriately intimidated judge and jury. Her ambition was marked by its nearly religious fervor, and in a way this was appropriate, for she had both her own and her parents' redemption to consider. Her passion was not so much for financial gain, though she looked forward to the day when her bank account would overflow, but rather for the return of her own (and, symbolically, her father's) sense of individual legitimacy and success.

Because she invested so much energy in keeping her two personas—public and private—alive and separate, it was to Kate's enormous advantage to keep a distance between herself and any potential partner. Though her relationship with Nick might have appeared to the untrained eye to resemble a close union—they did essentially live together—Kate did everything she could to conceal from Nick her true needs and desires. And in choosing to become involved with Nick, a person with less than functional communication skills and the emotional development of a gnat, Kate would be relatively secure in her knowledge that her innermost barriers would remain unpenetrated. It was only when he wearied of their mutual charade of domestic togetherness and actually started pursuing a more intimate kinship with her that it became necessary for her to bail out.

Kate can't get close to a man because doing so would require her to get closer to herself, to start seeing herself honestly. In the meantime, rather than take pride and satisfaction in the work she's done in reversing the setbacks life has dealt her, Kate can continue to sustain, her humiliation that these efforts are necessary at all. The only thing she feels about the realities of her present life—the financial aid, the student loans, the menial, low-paying jobs—is the passionate desire to put them behind her. True intimacy with a partner would make her feel trapped, because in order to be genuinely close to another person, she would have to admit to herself that her life was really that, the thing she was living, and she'd be forced to come face to face with the frustration and disappointment she works so hard not to feel. By relying on relationships that are no more than brief encounters, she can also maintain her distance from herself, safe in the fantasy that what she's living is a temporary purgatory, one from which, if she holds her breath long enough, she will emerge intact. Until she's willing to confront the reality in front of her and to see that her efforts to improve this reality have been Herculean, Kate will have to be satisfied with the joys of jurisprudence, because she won't be doing much dating.

If Kate gets involved with men who mistreat her, Lydia prefers men she can mistreat. Or at least that's how the men tell it. Lydia is what is classically known as a femme fatale, a woman about whom men lose their heads and to whom they often all too willingly sacrifice their hearts as well.

As an investment banker in an extremely male-dominated field, Lydia rubs elbows with a virtual sea of men; her workplace is teeming with them. And these men, most of them, really, really like Lydia. But then, what's not to like? Almost six feet tall, Lydia has glorious red hair that cascades down her back and cerulean blue eyes that are filled with mischief. She has also managed, in spite of her gender, to sustain a gradual ascension in her generally female-phobic company, so at age thirty, she has an impressive title to match her enviable measurements.

In spite of—or perhaps because of—her stunning appearance, Lydia hasn't had much luck sustaining long-term relationships. She claims she would like to, however, and many have been the briefly lucky gentlemen who for a time enjoyed her flattering attention. But no matter how handsome or charming (or rich, given her professional arena) a given man proves to be, Lydia simply cannot sustain her attraction for more than a few months. Sooner or later, her eye trails along to the next potential mate, and once this happens, Lydia tends not to stick around.

While the men around her tend to regard their work with the solemnity of brain surgery, Lydia takes a much more lighthearted and practical approach to professional life. She works hard, but at the end of the day, it's over. No crying over spilled S&L bonds, no jockeying for the admiration of her colleagues after a particularly choice deal—she gathers her belongings and disappears. While her coworkers are often mystified by her laissez faire attitude, she sees it this way: "I'm there to make money, nothing more, which I'm doing. The work itself doesn't especially interest me, and my ego's not all wrapped up in the deals I do, so I can't see the point in getting all freaked out about a job."

Lydia is, frankly, far more interested in social life. And, that being the case, it's fortunate that she has such an active one. A not atypical night for her involves meeting a beau after work for cocktails, racing off to meet another for a romantic dinner, and concluding the evening with the one she likes best, at that particular moment, for some dancing or a nightcap. And because she's decided that the final date of the evening is her favorite, he's the one she'll consent to escort her home.

Yes, it's true, Lydia sees a lot of action between the sheets. Unlike some other women to whom the idea of casual sex is anathema, she finds that she enjoys a pleasant romp most when she knows she's under no obligation to see her partner the next day— or at all, if that's what strikes her fancy. While she claims the idea of a steady beau appeals to her, one can't help but notice the care she takes in spacing a minimum number of days between trysts, so nobody gets too comfortable. And while this is a rule she has broken, in general she hasn't been particularly happy with the results.

For example: Around the time that I met her, Lydia was dating

Alex, a corporate attorney she'd met through her job. Alex was about ten years older than Lydia, devastating to look at and quite dashing to boot, pulling out chairs and lighting cigarettes like a modern-day Cary Grant; he was as gentlemanly and attentive to his date's friends as he was to his date. Lydia had been seeing Alex for about three months, and things appeared to be getting serious. Perhaps because of his advanced age, or perhaps because he recognized the prize before him, the dialogue between the two had turned rapidly from occasional get-togethers to full-fledged romance.

Alex wanted to get married, though he was too clever to reveal this overtly. He knew that extracting such a commitment from Lydia would require diplomacy and tact, and he took care not to rush her into any decisions. He did not, however, hesitate to whisk her off to exotic vacation locales for weekend getaways or accompany her to exclusive jewelry stores in order to purchase serious jewelry.

While Lydia was no stranger to extravagant pampering, even she was slightly awed by the silver-spoon treatment she was receiving at Alex's hands. Being picked up in his limousine and chauffeured to the airport at a moment's notice, dining at ambassador's homes, receiving her favorite flowers on an almost daily basis—Lydia couldn't help but find all of it thrilling. And while there were times when she felt a bit restless, or even bored, the arrival of Alex's personal masseuse would do wonders for her flagging spirit.

Lydia, by this point, had dated a lot of men; she had slept with a lot of men; and she knew one thing for certain: There was always something wrong with them. Not necessarily a big thing, not a deal breaker, just one or two quirks that would eventually come to irritate her. And as quirks went, Alex had comparatively few. He could be a bit stodgy, certainly, and he snored after a night of drinking, but relative to the advantages—his generosity and adoration—these were truly small complaints. Lydia knew she wanted to marry a successful and independent man—she couldn't stomach the thought of some starving artist toiling away on his "too good for this world" creations as he sucked her dry—and Alex was certainly a professional success. As the months passed, she became increasingly confident that when he finally broke down and popped the question, her answer would be yes.

So when Alex announced one morning over servant-prepared brioche and coffee that he'd been called away on business for a few days, Lydia looked forward to the time alone, getting organized, catching up with friends, and so forth. She was especially pleased when one of those friends mentioned she was having a get-together over the weekend and invited Lydia to attend. She plundered her closet for an appropriately festive outfit (noting that lately all she'd been wearing were over-tailored suits) and made an appointment to get her hair trimmed.

It had been a while since Lydia attended a social event without Alex on her arm, and during the cab ride over to her friend's apartment, she felt a familiar and somewhat thrilling tension rising in her. "It was strange," she explained later. "I felt like I was returning to myself, in a taxicab of all places. I was remembering who I was."

I've never met a woman—or a man, for that matter—immune to the very particular euphoria brought about by arriving at a social gathering with the understanding that all options are open. The possibility that you'll be noticed, admired, found charming and interesting—it's like a chance to be reborn into a better, more captivating self. And while you know there'll be a price to pay the next morning (that you'll feel something like Cinderella, after the ball but before the Prince returns to claim her, and with a rotten hangover to boot) it's nevertheless nearly impossible to suppress that magical surge of possibility.

For most people, such fleeting transformation is an occasional pleasure, not the basis of one's self-image but rather a sort of tantalizing icing on life's cake. Not so Lydia, for whom such social encounters were as endorphins are to marathon runners—essential, even addictive. As she sped south in her cab, Lydia recognized that this sense of expectation was something she had too long deferred, an utterly reaffirming experience of which she had been sorely deprived during her courtship with Alex.

When one enters a party in this sort of mood of confident anticipation, the odds are excellent that such mood will be rewarded. Intentional or not, when in this frame of mind one emanates a decidedly come-hither vibe, a kind of failproof radar received loud and clear by all prospective partners-in-flirting. And on this night, entering this soiree, Lydia found the shift from almost-married lady to temptingly single gadabout as easy as removing her ankle-length Lagerfeld coat. By the time she'd made her way across the room to the bar, greeting various friends en route, several men were queued up in anticipation, each proferring a cocktail intended solely for Lydia's refreshment.

To Lydia, the epigram "so many men, so little time" is not as laughably absurd as it might seem to those of us who reside in the ordinary (rather than the Claudia Schiffer) universe. On this particular night, there was a veritable platoon of men from whom Lydia might have chosen, any one of whom would have welcomed being so chosen with the delirium usually reserved for bull's-eye lottery numbers. Lydia took advantage of her over-full dance card, flitting from man to man, all of whom enjoyed the attractive (to Lydia) distinction of being complete strangers to her. To paraphrase David Mamet, Lydia liked men, she liked all men, but she especially liked men she didn't know very well.

As soon as she laid eyes on Nate, she knew she'd found her dish. Five or six years her junior, Nate possessed the surly, ruinous sex appeal of a young Marlon Brando and, given his habit of drinking scotch straight from the bottle, was most likely disposed of a similar temperament as well. A corporeal incarnation of the word *challenge*, Nate circled the room in gradual descent upon Lydia, who coolly feigned ignorance of him. When he opened his mouth — a mouth to which the corrective possibility of dental work had plainly remained a stranger—and out poured a charmingly cockney accent, Lydia knew she'd hit pay dirt.

Lydia had spent the last six months sitting primly beside Alex while he sampled wine for anxious maître'd's, so Nate's invitation to follow him out to the fire escape and share some of his firewater was extremely tantalizing. She knew mention of hostile corporate takeovers or darling little villas in St. Bartholomew would not darken their conversation's door; Nate's expertise would likely include famous soccer riots or Charles Bronson movies. Lydia was in heaven.

Nate, his long legs swinging from the rusted wrought-iron grate on which they perched, was that intoxicating blend of gruff and enigmatic; he was the kind of guy who's slow to reveal his intentions, if indeed he has any. Unlike all the others inside clamoring for her phone number, Nate would make Lydia work to keep his attention. And this was exactly the way she liked it, for where was the victory in winning a fixed game? Furthermore, Nate's reticence forced Lydia to stretch the boundaries of herself, becoming more charming and beguiling than even she'd have thought possible. So when Nate finally set his bottle down in order to kiss her, she felt she'd truly earned the gesture, that she'd been evaluated and deemed worthy.

And so began Lydia's double life. It was not the first time her existence had split down the middle and likely not the last. This time, however, the fact that she was actually living with Alex made the logistics of her deception slightly more complicated. Still, she couldn't seem to make herself forswear the wild, expansive excitement she felt whenever in Nate's presence, just as the idea of giving up Alex's lavish and comforting attention seemed impossible to abide.

During her assignations with Nate, Lydia felt free of all the petty, diminishing constraints of womanly good behavior. No staid, snooty cocktail parties, no evenings listening to Mozart at Lincoln Center—Nate met her in ever seedier bars, never hesitating to drag his beloved motorcycle right along with him. He would frequently disappear into the bowels of the establishment, to play pool or buy drugs—Lydia couldn't be sure what he was up to as she shifted on her bar stool, buying her own drinks and warding off the artless advances of the bar's other patrons. Still, when he returned and slung his arm across her back, she felt thrilled to have made claim to this wild man even briefly.

Meanwhile, back at the ranch, Alex was becoming increasingly disgruntled by Lydia's mysterious behavior, her sudden need to head out mid-evening, her last-minute canceling of dinnertime engagements. And though she was initially intent on sustaining her carefully orchestrated duplicity, Alex's possessiveness and complaints gradually began to irritate her, propelling her into less cautious behavior. On a night when she knew Alex had plans that would keep him occupied until after midnight, she decided to entertain Nate right at home.

"Nate was such a naughty experience in general," she explained later, "and I thought bringing him into my and Alex's house would heighten that somehow. I guess I just wanted to see how bad I could really be." She learned precisely that when Alex surprised Lydia and her date by arriving home early, his engagement having been cut short by his host's poor health. At the zenith of the ensuing confrontation, Alex threw a Baccarat decanter at Nate, at which point Nate wisely decided to take his leave, scuttling out of the apartment like a crab.

Alex wasn't interested in hearing an explanation of Lydia's indiscretion or listening to her apologies, perhaps sensing how half-hearted these sentiments would be. What he was interested in was watching Lydia pack her things and leave, which she did. She checked into a hotel and settled onto the bed, no doubt wondering if it was worth a call to Nate to see if he'd like to join her.

"I do feel bad about Alex," Lydia noted shortly after their split, while we sat in her beige hotel room poring over the real estate section of the newspaper. Though she claimed she wanted to find an apartment, it was apparent that she was not suffering for her stay at the hotel, clearly relishing the plush anonymity of her temporary surroundings. "He's been absolutely ice cold to me, ever since that night. But I know it's because he feels terrible, and he doesn't want to show it."

She leaned back into her overstuffed chair and took a sip of cappuccino. "But the truth is, I'm not sorry it's over. I would have ended it differently, given the choice, less cruelly. But I see now that I was suffocating." Many of us might have found a way to adapt to this sort of oxygen deprivation, complete as it was with the solicitude of hired help and an unlimited wardrobe allowance. And while we've all heard horror stories about material-driven women being bought by overly controlling men who systematically undermine their self-esteem and ruin their lives, Alex happened not to be a member of this particular fraternity. He delighted in Lydia's independence and dedication to her career and had plenty of interests of his own—both social and professional—to keep him occupied.

Lydia's dissatisfaction could not be attributed to any particular behavior or attitude of Alex's. The problem was far more fundamental, involving the very existence of Alex or anyone like him. No matter how ideal a particular mate might appear to be, once the word *mate* applied to him, the air around Lydia started getting awfully thin. After the demise of her relationship with Alex, she continued to date Nate but conceded that she knew this courtship would remain a casual and occasional sexual friendship.

Lydia contends that she would like to meet someone and marry, to eventually have children. She continues to date aggressively, apparently seeking involvement with a man who'll fit her specific bill. But whenever a given partnership begins to get serious, she invariably gets itchy, restless, and sooner or later she ends up in somebody else's bed.

At this point in her life, Lydia cannot give up the tremendous satisfaction of being viewed through a fresh pair of eyes, the sense of personal possibility that being seen anew inspires in her. To commit to one person, to accept that this person's vision of her, coupled with her own, would comprise the total picture of her identity, feels like surrender to her, like resignation to a life of arrested motion, options evaporating like dry-ice smoke after a Black Sabbath concert. And before she can begin to bridge the distance between the domestic life she claims she desires and her inability to tolerate the merest notion of romantic fidelity, Lydia will likely have to examine her ongoing need for the possibility of personal transformation. Chances are, once she does, she will have to confront the probability that it is she, rather than the men she keeps ejecting, who is not measuring up to her own prodigiously high standards.

My brilliant and long-suffering editor has begged me to curb my compulsion to relate the family histories to which I have been perennially drawn while profiling the women in this book. "Live in the present," she urges sensibly, blithely unaware of the deceptive difficulty of such a command. "I will, I will," I grumble, wishing once again that everyone shared my feeling that the truly important events of one's life occur between birth and age ten, and that any mystery about a person can be solved simply by spending fifteen minutes observing his or her family.

In the case of Cynthia, it would be an exercise in futility to disregard the effects of the formative years of her existence. Her early life had the sort of plot to which first novelists are drawn for its undiluted version of pathos and melodrama. And while I know this is a book about commitment anxiety rather than lousy childhoods, I believe strongly that the lessons Cynthia learned in her early years are the basis of her commitment phobia today.

The child of Mexican immigrants, Cynthia grew up in Southern California. Her parents had emigrated as teenagers from the tiny, impoverished village in which they were born and arrived in the United States with high hopes. However, the difficulties of language acquisition and job scarcity made their dreamed-of assimilation all too elusive. Instead of recasting themselves as our century's version of the petit bourgeois—convenience store owners—and saving to send their children to Harvard, Cynthia's parents began a kind of inexorable downslide into economic ruin, and worse.

By the time they began to have children, the situation was bleak. Cynthia's father, the primary breadwinner, had stumbled upon the temporary and persuasive succor of drugs, progressing rapidly from the occasional bag of marijuana to the far less occasional bag of heroin. When he was high, her father was kind and genial, if a bit distracted. But when his chemical cheer began to wear off, what replaced it was kind of grisly panic—that is, until the next supply was purchased. Because money was at constant issue, it often fell to Cynthia and her sisters to scrounge for money, borrowing it from irritated neighbors or indulging in petty thievery. As a tiny child, these episodes were a source of horrendous shame for Cynthia, who even then understood something about the social contract and the delight bystanders took in pernicious judgments.

While her father was enthusiastically engaged in a private cycle of binge and recovery, her mother had her own method of checking out. While she didn't physically abandon the family, she did retreat into a vivid world of fantasy, where things like your toddler stumbling upon her father shooting up in the bathroom don't happen. Because her own family, unlike her husband's, had been moderately comfortable in Mexico, and she had made the decision to leave that life purely out of love for her new mate, Cynthia's mother did not possess the drive to succeed or the fortitude that paves the way for so many new arrivals to this country.

So these were the options presented to Cynthia as a child: One could either choose the alternate euphoria and anguish of addiction or retreat into a happiness that had no relationship to the actual world around her. Cynthia opted for a little of each. Although she loathed the chemical oblivion for which her father constantly hungered, she nevertheless developed a passion for the idea of escape. Her mother's version, however badly it translated into making life manageable or caring for one's family, was considerably more palatable to her. She remembers sitting for hours while her mother gathered her girls around her, reminiscing exaggeratedly about her own idyllic girlhood or fantasizing about the unlimited glory of her daughters' futures.

Cynthia took her mother's fantasies to heart. Despite the fact that the family rarely had enough money to buy groceries or pay the electric bill, she devoted herself furiously to the idea of a better life. She attacked her schoolwork with a mania and, when she wasn't studying, tracked down as many paying jobs as she could find. By the time she was twenty-four, she had put herself through college and had landed a decently paying job working as a paralegal for an enormous law firm.

Naturally, when I first met Cynthia, I knew nothing of her past. What I did know was that she was friendly and amiable and that I coveted her gorgeous mane. Cynthia is blessed with a head of black hair of the sort that compels Irish girls to visit their priests, forced to confess the sin of envy. So thick and glossy are her tresses, hanging heavy as a velvet curtain, you could apply your lipstick in their reflection. Cynthia is quite tall, and she holds herself with a kind of square-shouldered dignity. Words like *comportment* and *carriage* come easily when describing her, and indeed her outward composure is something she very deliberately maintains. And while it's apparent that her organization and efficiency helped her transcend her troubled early years, it takes some time to see that what also fueled her progress toward a remade life was the wild-spiritedness just beneath her poised exterior.

Throughout her life, Cynthia hasn't had much trouble attracting men. She has had trouble, however, reciprocating the romantic interests of any but the most manipulative and emotionally selfish of these men. She recognizes this inclination in herself; she knows that her taste leads her where no woman would sanely go, but go there she does, and repeatedly. In theory, Cynthia would like to meet a man equal to her in intelligence and emotional generosity, someone with whom she could build a life of mutual interests and satisfactions. In reality, her boyfriends tend to be drinking beer in front of the television at ten A.M., wondering when Cynthia's going to get around to making breakfast, or if she'll agree to make a quick stop at the OTB on her way to the office.

Unlike many women who become delusional at the onset of a relationship, convincing themselves their new partner is the Second Coming, only to realize three months later that they're dating a modern-day Charles Manson, Cynthia tends to make absolutely accurate assessments of the men on whom she sets her sights. She sees that they're beyond rehabilitation, set in their patterns of self-absorption with virtually no desire to change. She understands that this is their attraction for her.

"I tell myself all the time that I must be crazy, because the moment I meet one of these guys, I know what the future will be. I've certainly lived through it enough times to know. But there's something in their irresponsibility, a kind of freedom, that I'm drawn to. Because however involved I get, however much I start to care, I know that these guys basically don't. And I guess I must want to be more like that."

It's hard to achieve clarity when you're constantly running out for fresh six-packs of Schlitz and avoiding phone calls from your boyfriend's creditors, but Cynthia's remarks reveal more than she realizes. She does want something these men have, and it's not their compulsive untidiness or inability to fill out unemployment insurance applications. Cynthia wants their freedom. For her, such freedom represents the same relief and happiness she found in the escapist fantasies of her childhood.

She has attempted, a few times, to become involved in the sort of relationship she imagines she ultimately wants. She's dated, albeit briefly, men capable of appreciating her attributes, of participating emotionally in the partnership, of sustaining gainful employment. And while she's momentarily pleased by these unions, knowing that (unlike her other variety) there's the possibility of connection and a future, it's not terribly long before she starts itching to get out. Because the one thing this woman who can tolerate nearly any kind of domestic unpleasantness or exploitation cannot abide is having the full attention of a lover. To be seen—not simply in terms of how she looks in a thong bikini but to have her presence and particular identity register with a man she's involved with—makes Cynthia feels absolutely trapped. She worries about her unhealthy predilection for vice-addicts and losers, but this is merely a symptom of the real issue. The miscreants with whom Cynthia routinely becomes involved are simply incapable of focusing their bloodshot eyes on the reality of who she is, and so with them she is able to maintain her perfect, inviolate, interior freedom.

Cynthia grew up believing that the split between reality and fantasy was as critical a distinction as the one between life and death. And, to be sure, her escape from the wretched environment provided by her mother's compulsive quixotry probably did save Cynthia's life—at least her spiritual life—once or twice. The problem is that, while she has indeed managed to create a legitimately better world for herself, she cannot stand the thought of wholly inhabiting this place because of her gruesome associations with the concept of real life. Similarly, getting and staying involved with someone worth the effort would mean that her partner would act as a sort of mirror in which she would have to see herself clearly. And, doing so, she could no longer sustain the fantasy life that allows her such complete detachment from herself and her experiences.

As I've said, Cynthia has known precisely what she was getting into with every disastrous relationship. In order to maintain the illusion that she could be absolutely anything, that change of every kind was always possible, she needed to choose men who weren't capable of or interested in making an assessment of her, whose vision was obscured by more immediate concerns, such as getting the Kentucky Fried Chicken container open before its contents turned soggy. In Cynthia's mind, to be a known quantity was to be a static quantity, someone for whom the shift to an increasingly better existence would no longer be possible.

Still, she is optimistic. She's beginning to understand more clearly the need to reconcile fantasy with reality and to learn through experience—her platonic friendships, the satisfaction she takes from her work, her efforts to create a pleasant and inviting home for herself—that fantasy can make reality better and more appealing and that she doesn't have to work so hard to keep the two separate. Once she fully accepts this fact, the idea of a steady, solid partner will no longer seem so threatening, and she'll be sending the crew of romantic pinheads back to the poppy fields from which they came.

As reluctant grown-ups, we've all at one time or another experienced a kind of shocked outrage at the mundane reality of our lives, especially compared to the glorious fantasies of future adulthood that kept us afloat during our adolescence. When we were fourteen and listening to Queen's "Bohemian Rhapsody" over and over on our inexpensive American-made stereo systems, all we had to do to keep from shoving our heads in the oven was imagine ourselves ten years in the future: decorating our chic but affordable studio apartments with batik curtains and Ansel Adams prints, standing before full-length mirrors in small-print rayon dresses and waiting for our doorbell to be buzzed by our date for the evening, having an entire kitchen cabinet devoted solely to the storage of top-shelf liquor.

So it comes as a bit of a shock to realize that adult life has less to do with turning down high-profile anchorwoman stints and jetting off to Paris for long weekends than it does with resignedly setting our alarm clocks for seven A.M. so we won't arrive late at our low-paying secretarial jobs. No Audrey Hepburn vanilla linen cigarette pants and breakfast at Tiffany's for us, more like our fathers' cast-off flannel pajamas and Stouffer's Lean Cuisine.

And if we have trouble reconciling the outer trappings of our sometimes less-than-glamorous existences, it's even more of a challenge to come to terms with the disappointments we may have with the people we've actually become rather than our childhood fantasies of who we would be. So challenging, in fact, that we sometimes turn to a strenuous kind of denial or rejection of that person we know ourselves to actually be. And when this is the case, when we refuse reality and let ourselves get caught up in fantasy, it makes a certain kind of sense that intimate, committed relationships are not a viable possibility. If in order to tolerate your life, you need to cultivate the belief that profound change and personal transformation are always just around the corner, the last thing you want is the albatross of a genuine relationship, the kind that demands a certain reconciliation to the truth of who you are and a willingness to reveal and share that self.

If one's primary commitment is to the idea that metamorphosis into an acceptable self is minutes away, commitments of a more interpersonal nature are simply not going to happen. Whether you find the parameters of your adult life intolerable, whether you need to rediscover yourself compulsively through the eyes of romantic others, or whether you haven't figured out yet that fantasy is not a replacement for, but rather an enhancement of, reality—if any or all of these conditions sound familiar, chances are you'll remain something of a stranger to true and satisfying love.

PART 3

10

The Fabulous Commitment Quiz

Second only to my passion for celebrity murder trials is my love of those quizzes that routinely appear in women's magazines. In case you've been spending all your time in a cave with the Dead Sea Scrolls, rather than on your convertible sofa bed reading issues of *Cosmopolitan*, those mini-questionnaires are designed to furnish their respondents with an increased self-knowledge. Depending on the nature of the quiz, we are given opportunity to discover all manner of secret, venal facts about ourselves, such as precisely how bone-lazy we really are (despite all our efforts to simulate the illusion of industry) or what the likelihood is that our profligate spending habits will lead us to a life of full-scale criminal activity. But mostly these quizzes are intended to illuminate us as to our disastrous inclinations when it comes to love.

Just by cozying up on the couch with a pen in hand or huddling in a cold stall of the office ladies' room, we are rewarded with succinct and penetrating insight into the shadowy nether regions of our psyches—a veritable road map of our hidden impulses. And unlike those other maps crammed with illegibly printed street names, nobody's going to scream at us in a claustrophobic, over-heated car if we happen to overlook the approach of a critical free-way exit.

So go hunt down a writing implement, pour yourself a drink, and settle down to answer the following questions.

1) You enter a party, heart aflutter with anticipation, and con-fident that your thigh-length Lycra undergarment has honored its advertising and succeeded in removing literal inches from your "problem area." A quick survey of the room informs you that there are at least three single men in attendance. Toward which do you head?

a) The solitary fellow sitting on the carpet, arms and legs akimbo, surreptitiously pouring himself a tall glass of scotch from the bottle he's hiding behind the leg of a chair.

b) The gentlemen engaged in conspicuous appreciation of your bustline, even as he partakes of a tender slow dance with another female guest.

c) The cute guy in the backward baseball cap who's been smiling shyly at you across the room, in between his casual perusals of your host's overstocked bookshelves.

2) You've enjoyed three dates with an exceedingly attractive, compelling, and decidedly mysterious man. Enjoyed them despite the fact that the man in question arrived an hour and a half late to collect you for your last assignation. Now it's the night of your eagerly awaited fourth date, and it appears that he's not planning to show at all. You:

a) Decide that this is a romance not meant to be. Turn the answering machine on, slip anything by Merchant-Ivory into the VCR, and make yourself an enormous bowl of buttered popcorn. Climb into bed and watch the movie, imagining yourself in every outfit you see on the screen. If and when the phone does ring, ignore it.

b) Get hysterical and call five girlfriends, one after the other. Spend three hours on the telephone analyzing the potential implications of your date's failure to appear. Wonder if it's worth a couple of quick calls to some area hospitals.

c) Distract yourself by making a list of the children's names that best compliment your nondate's surname.

3) The man you've been seeing for three months—whom you've tried, without success, to find a reason to despise—suddenly suggests that you give up your apartment and come to live with him. You respond by:

a) Selling all your belongings and applying for entrance to the witness relocation program.

b) Telling him that, while it's probably a bit too soon to change addresses, you'd be happy to commandeer one drawer of his dresser for your overnight essentials.

c) Getting drunk and seducing his best friend.

4) You're enjoying an evening out with friends, and for some perplexing and wonderful reason men keep approaching to offer you drinks and invite you to dance. By the evening's end, two tenacious fellows are vying rather touchingly for your attention. You discover that one of these men, Mike, lives nearly two hundred miles away and is in town for the weekend visiting friends. The other, Ike, owns an apartment five blocks south of yours. As the evening draws to a close, you:

a) Surreptitiously place your hand on Mike's knee and ask him if it's true, as you've been told, that the cocktail lounge of his hotel makes the best martinis in the city.

b) Suggest that Mike run and fetch you another drink and, while he's gone, discreetly jot your telephone number inside Ike's matchbook.

c) Gaze moonily at Mike and ask him to describe his city—a city you've never visited nor wanted to, as you've imagined it to be the dreariest place on earth. As he does, fantasize irrationally and rhapsodically about what it would be like to live there.

5) You've been slaving away on your version of the Great American Novel for five long years, bravely keeping hope alive even as you're forced to wait tables to pay the rent. Your parents, whose once-high hopes are steadily spiraling downward, have commented that if they'd chosen to have a bonfire with your college tuition money, at least they would have kept warm. Suddenly your Red Sea parts in the form of an offer from a major publishing house. When the man you've been seeing telephones, you:

a) Demand that he rush over immediately to take you out for a ridiculously expensive celebration dinner. Tell him to plan on spending the night.

b) Inform him that one of the conditions of your book contract is that you move immediately to Manhattan, in order that you can be available for impromptu editorial meetings with your publisher. Promise to write as soon as you're settled.

c) Affect a Scottish accent and assure him snottily that he's dialed the wrong number.

6) A killingly attractive colleague whom you've long worshiped from afar, whose every move you've obsessively chronicled for those exhausted friends who are actually still willing take your calls, a man who, were he slightly more observant, could easily have you con-

victed on stalking charges, appears before you suddenly at the office Christmas party and inquires as to whether he can offer you a cocktail. Your first instinct is to:

a) Pretend you don't understand English.

b) Officiously inform him—this despite the empty wineglass dangling from your fingers—that you never drink alcohol.

c) Hand him your glass and, grinning, tell him, "I'll have whatever you're having."

7) Dressing for work one morning, you slip on the dress carefully selected the night before from the "fat" section of your closet and notice that the seams are beginning to strain. You begin randomly ripping garments from hangers, growing ever more frantic until you suddenly understand why Karen Carpenter suffered a fatal heart attack in her closet. When you finally arrive at work, late, you are greeted by the sound of your boss bellowing your name. Upon returning to your desk, having endured your chastisement, you settle before your typewriter and briefly contemplate the several, apparently meaningless academic degrees you've earned, before setting about to work.

After eight long hours of clerical tasks, just as escape seems possible, you're reminded that your attendance is required at an important client function. Gritting your teeth, you compose yourself and set off for the party. When you arrive, you immediately:

a) Conspicuously circle the room, greeting clients in the most effusive and public way possible. Locate the partially hidden back exit and glide smoothly toward it. Out on the street, flag down a cab and hightail it to your boyfriend's apartment for a little much-deserved special attention.

b) Sidle up to the band and attempt eye contact with the drug-glazed, tattoo-happy, altogether mirthless drummer.

c) Smile bewitchingly at a fellow guest whose menacing demeanor leads you to suspect he has a weapon concealed beneath his ill-fitting sportcoat. Listen attentively as he regales you with his complex and highly nuanced conspiracy theories. When he abruptly decides to take his leave, offer to accompany him.

8) Your best gay male friend, a brilliant but undiscovered clothing designer whom you wasted several crucial years being in love with, implores you to join him at a chic fashion industry party. Though you know most of the revelers at this particular soiree will be gay men, thus assuring you of a romance-free evening, you consent to keep your pal company. You arrive at the gala and quickly down a glass of champagne. All of a sudden:

a) You decide that perhaps you've been rash in assuming that *all* of your exceedingly well-dressed and sublimely buffed fellow guests exclusively prefer the company of men.

b) You begin to skillfully eavesdrop on the group of men standing right behind you. Overhear two of the men lightheartedly teasing the third about his heterosexuality, using phrases such as "out of your element." Shift position and discreetly ascertain whether there's anything to get worked up about. Decide there is. Take a step toward the threesome and smile, extending your hand.

c) You notice that the bartender is a dead ringer for Michelangelo's *David*. Deciding that you can't live in a world where men this gaspingly beautiful prefer pectorals to breasts, you spend the next forty minutes attempting to get his telephone number until finally he slumps into a chair, head in his hands, and begs you to leave him alone.

9) It's April and everyone's spirits are buoyed by the suddenly warm weather. Your boyfriend cheerfully asks whether you want to

join him and some friends in the rental of a summer cottage for the month of July. You:

    a) Stare at him incredulously and bitterly whisper, "What makes you think we'll even know each other in July?"

    b) Open your checkbook and ask, "How much?"

    c) Tell him you'd love to, but you're pretty sure the mole on your shoulder is inoperable melanoma, so the chances are good that, by July, you'll be dead.

10) Your boyfriend, an angelic fellow whom you've been living with for years, starts dropping not-so-coy hints about a big surprise he's planning. While he's not looking, you rifle through his wallet and, sure enough, find a jewelry store receipt inside. Per his instructions, you meet him the following evening at a fancy French restaurant. Upon arriving you:

    a) Frantically begin to accuse him—based on absolutely no evidence—of having an affair. Convince yourself that his astonished protestations are proof of his guilt. Storm out of the restaurant alone, weeping loudly.

    b) Scowl when he hands you a small velvet box. Open it and examine the contents silently. Snap it shut and hand it back to him, commenting primly, "I guess my mother was right. We really *do* have different taste."

    c) Sip a glass of champagne nervously, waiting for your man to make his move. Silently practice the word *yes*. When he reaches into his pocket and extracts the "surprise," finish practicing and start talking.

11

Key to the Fabulous Commitment Quiz

ABSOLUTELY BEST POSSIBLE ANSWERS: 1) c, 2) a, 3) b, 4) b, 5) a, 6) c, 7) a, 8) b, 9) b, 10) c.

If you selected three or more of the above answers to the preceding questions, you have an excellent shot at transcending the commitment phobia that has until now controlled your every waking moment.

If not—and I'm sorry to be the one to break this news—then you're spending way too much time sprinting at hard-hearted windmills who are never going to show up on time for a date or consent to meet your parents. At the risk of sounding like a high school gym teacher, it's time to stop kidding yourself. You want a boyfriend about as much as you want anesthetic-free open-heart surgery. And so what? Better that you should worry about what you do want right now and figure out how to get it. Because love's not planning to show up until you're good and ready.

12

Conclusion

THE MOST OBVIOUS DRAWBACK to being female is the fact that women have a greater percentage of natural body fat than do men. This means, in rough scientific translation, that most men can eat like pigs at a trough and stay thin as beans, whereas we are bound to a life spent scanning grocery shelves for a reduced-fat salad dressing that tastes like something other than boiled tap water. And when one adds to this hardship all the other obstacles our gender faces—the dreary management of water retention; the difficulty of receiving with equanimity the news that our male coworkers are paid on a different, and higher, scale than we; the realization that epidurals sometimes fail—one is forced to wonder whether being a woman is really worth the trouble.

Nobody needs to remind women that the zeitgeist of matriarchy is millennia past or that the mantle of cultural dominion has been usurped by men. To avoid becoming fixated on this injustice, it's often useful to approach one's gender from a different angle, to focus on the subtler benefits of being a member of, as Sartre's squeeze Simone de Beauvoir put it, "The Second Sex." Instead of concentrating on the fact that we're not exactly in charge and did not make the particular rules we're expected to live by, we have the option of viewing these rules with a certain clear-eyed objectivity and, if we're in the right mood, a bit of healthy sedition. They're not our rules, after all, so our investment in protecting their sanctity could accurately be described as nil.

But there's one cultural assumption that seems to be exempt from the usual female skepticism. It's the doctrine that suggests that women are not worth very much without rings on our fingers—and don't insult me by asking which finger I mean. We women are suckers for this kind of lunacy. I'm serious; ask the strongest woman about her romantic status and she'll likely turn into a pod person— an automaton who mechanically raises her hand so we can admire the cut of her stone, or an apologist who shamefacedly admits that she's still single. Women tend to have this troubling knee-jerk reaction whenever the word *relationship* is uttered. (Also dangerous are the phrases *Waterford crystal* and *place settings for twelve.*) Brain surgeon or astronaut, no matter her accomplishments, confront a woman with the subject of romantic success and all that it signifies (marriage! children!) and she'll likely find herself agreeing that such commitment is the raison d'être of every female alive.

Whereas in response to other offending cultural attitudes we'll climb aboard foul-smelling buses and travel to protest marches or cackle with derisive laughter during elegant dinner parties, when it comes to the subject of mating, we still refuse to question the received wisdom that those among our sisters who reject the role of conjugal helpmeet are irredeemable freaks. Even nuns, after all, marry Jesus, although one imagines that the division of household labor in that arrangement leaves something to be desired.

In light of our apparent unwillingness to question the conventional attitude concerning women and commitment, why do we so regularly veer off the consecrated, prescribed path toward the validation that such commitment guarantees? We avoid or sabotage relationships or, if we're not capable of such directness, we simply seek out partners who we know will orchestrate the destruction of our couplings, thereby permitting us the face-saving role of romantic victim—which, given the alternative roles of heretic or pariah, really isn't such a bad option.

So what gives? How do we explain this discrepancy in our romantic behavior? Admittedly, it's a paradox that might not immediately strike us as monumental, except when we consider the disproportionate space the subject occupies in our addled little minds. Since we refuse to openly challenge our society's requirement of pairing up like Noah's animals, why has our commitment phobia become such a widespread closet epidemic?

I believe that the anxiety women feel about commitment is rooted in our anxiety about ourselves. We are in the midst of an identity crisis, and the source of that crisis is the conflict that's arisen as a result of being told that we are now equal members of a culture that does it's damnedest to severely restrict the parameters of what it considers acceptable female behavior. In other words, whether we're winning the school spelling bee or heading the oncology department of a world-renowned teaching hospital, females understand that we are still expected to be warm and solicitious, empathetic and noncompetitive. Nice—women are expected to be nice. Anger, frustration, outrage, irritation, pragmatism, coolness—the list of responses considered inappropriate for women is as long as Kim Basinger's legs.

Because women continue to be held to a standard of good behavior that is reductive and outdated (and, frankly, delusional), we're forbidden access to the spectrum of responses and actions that make it possible to exist in these new realms, be they the workplace or the playing field. We're like soldiers who have been instructed to show up for a battle without guns. Patriarchy has permitted us entry into its consecrated province, but on the strict condition of enforced impotency.

Anyone who has ever held a job knows the drill: A man who

comfortably inhabits and openly values his position of power is generally regarded as a role model, ardently admired for his ambition and ability to remain focused. But when a woman is put in an identical position, her efforts to effectively do her job may soon brand her as an unmitigated, castrating bitch. She may have gained entry to the man's world, but the complete and natural spectrum of responses to that world—responses that are available to, even required of, men—remain verboten to her. However high women climb on the corporate ladder, however many award-winning buildings we design or successful bone marrow transplants we perform, it's still mandatory that our undertakings be accompanied by sweet and obliging smiles.

In my experience, women are less afraid of romantic intimacy per se than they are implications of such intimacy. Implicit in romantic intimacy is the willingness to make ourselves available to our lovers. And before we can do this, we need to be prepared to acknowledge exactly who it is we're offering up to that old jokester Eros. True and enduring commitment is not a step we can take without at least a modicum of self-knowledge. Which wouldn't be such an alarming proposition if such knowledge did not require investigation into parts of ourselves we've done our best to keep as hidden away as Bertha Rochester in her attic. With comparably unpleasant results.

While profiling the women in this book, myself included, I've returned repeatedly to the theme of intimacy, both the intimacy we can effect with one's partner as well as our capacity for intimacy with ourselves. Whether they are tossing their creative work in the path of increased romantic closeness (as in the case of Isabel or Kate), or short-circuiting incipient—and perfectly good—relationships by jumping into bed with anybody new (Lydia), by falling prey to the allure of gay men (Annie), or by obsessing about fantastical physical flaws (Elizabeth), the ways in which these women avoid closeness is less important than the fact that they do. Because the two are inextricably connected: A fear of intimacy with one's mate is almost always related to a fear of intimacy with oneself. And if the core of commitment anxiety is a fear of oneself, the same self we've been carting around since the day we managed to get ourselves born, then what precisely is there to be afraid of?

Plenty. Because, and this is especially true of women, once we begin to establish an intimate, honest relationship with ourselves, once we're capable of viewing ourselves fully, we are then forced to confront the fact that we are, as Whitman put it, "large, and contain multitudes." This involves accepting our entire selves—our inclination to be loving and kind, pleasant and generous, as well as our moments of competitiveness and irritability, selfishness and rage. But such acceptance is far from easy when we live in a world that really hates it when we fail to conceal our feelings of hostility or despair. To do so is the equivalent of getting drunk and passing out at one's own party. We should know better, dammit.

Learning to acknowledge and become comfortable with our "bad girl" impulses is enormously difficult when such impulses are uniformly met with disgust and outrage, when the notion of positive reinforcement is a pipe dream on the grandest scale. Men weren't fooling around when they conjured up the division between angels and whores, a paradigm that demonstrates rather succinctly the ominous consequences of stepping on the cracks of female good behavior. Women recognize (some of us from hard-won experience, others from observation) the "one false move" aspect of this particular morality tale; we know that even a single misstep while navigating the angel-whore distinction goes directly into our permanent file, and it's a black mark far more damning than our youthful acts of cutting geometry class or shoplifting drugstore cosmetics. The division between bad and good girls, regardless of our evolving cultural consciousness, has remained surprisingly neat and static.

How do women respond to this expectation? On the surface, most of us react by becoming extremely cooperative. We try—hard—

to be nice. We are solicitous of people at dinner parties who seem shier than we, we juggle our schedules to accommodate the needs of colleagues or friends, we force ourselves to remember before planning menus if anyone's a vegetarian. But the not-nice parts of women don't just completely evaporate; even the constraints of good behavior aren't that powerful. Instead, the sedition, the anger, the crankiness and impatience simply go underground. They get hidden. But they continue to exist. Some might even say they get stronger, kind of like those sinister-looking roots that one finds growing out of potatoes stored too long under the sink. However well we might manage our appearance of benign geniality, there's plenty of subversive activity beneath our exfoliated surfaces.

As a rule, the women I know are far more secretive and willful and intolerant of authority than are any of the men I've met. I instinctively resisted this conclusion for a long time, so poorly did it fit into the conventional picture I'd assumed was accurate. Don't get me wrong: These women, myself included, were awfully well behaved. They just weren't what you'd describe as nice. But nice is a quality you look for in cows or wildflowers. For friends, and yourself, you want something a bit more interesting and complex. Isn't the whole point of enduring childhood—all those hours spent dodging sadistic physical education teachers and memorizing algebraic formulas that had virtually no future application—the knowledge that when we finally pass through the golden gates of adulthood, we can behave in absolutely any lawful way we like?

Sure, if you happen to be a man. But for women, the rewards of entering the kingdom of adulthood are slightly more obscured. Because the moment a woman begins to exhibit anything other than cheerful pliability, she encounters a criticism festival, a condemnation free-for-all. Open yourself up to this public stoning a few times and you'll learn that, if you're a woman, you had better quickly master the art of suppression. And once you do, the female-perfected division between public amenability and private dissension is cemented.

So what bearing does all of this have on our hidden agenda of relationship avoidance? The division between public and private that occurs in women is directly related to our attraction to unavailable or inappropriate partners, or our circumvention of romantic activity altogether, because the very condition of intimacy presumes disclosure of parts of us we believe we must never reveal. And yet even as we may regret our rebellious and nonconforming impulses, we are protective of them as well. We've come to believe that, in order to keep intact those parts of ourselves we've submerged, we need to maintain a distance from anyone who might ask us to change. We fear that if we divulge the characteristics that define our private selves, they'll be co-opted, re-formed into something presentable and dead. We're prepared to be Stepford Wives only to a certain point, and the sacrifice of our private responses and attitudes is not included in the social contract we signed.

However tempting the prospect of meaningful communion with a romantic partner may be, our fear that such communion will mean the surrender of those parts of us that make us whole forces us (sometimes consciously, sometimes not) to place impediments in the path of potential closeness. We date criminals or married men, we attempt to date homosexuals, we avoid social life altogether, and we do so not because we're insane or stupid, but because we're afraid of the consequences of full disclosure to our mates.

As I've said before, women's disinclination to engage in intimate romantic involvement would be perfectly fine if it weren't for the horrendous anxiety and despair we feel whenever we have to purchase a wedding present for someone other than ourselves or check the box marked "single" on standardized forms. If our lack of involvement in a relationship could be an acceptable condition, like the inability to digest milk, then our lives would be radically different. If a solitary Saturday night weren't a source of blinding anguish, if we didn't spend so much valuable time and energy obsessing about our encounters with men or absence of same, it's fairly clear that women might be both a great deal happier and considerably more productive. Try to imagine the results if all the innumerable hours you've spent on the telephone or stretched across some girlfriend's chintz bedspread compulsively dissecting your latest love disaster were used for some other task: writing a million-dollar screenplay, teaching yourself to speak French, reading the classics, learning to play the stock market and, once you've mastered it, sending yourself on a world tour with all the windfall. Or even just figuring out what you want to do with your life and how you can bring this goal to fruition.

I'm all for love. I just wish I'd recognized during all those years spent in its crazed and conflicted pursuit that I simply wasn't prepared to handle the actual experience of it. And I wasn't ready because I knew so little about who I was—a process that I severely impeded by focusing my attention on every question but the one concerning my own identity. All of this was, of course, not an accident. I was afraid to confront the truth of who I was because I knew I was teeming with fractious, unacceptable qualities, and knowing this, I had not a clue about what to do with this information. Recognizing that I did not correspond to the model of feminine virtue I observed nearly everywhere around me, I feared that I was as damaged as a manufacturer's second. It took a great many things (experience, an increasing unwillingness to lie to myself, the help of a brilliant and sagacious therapist, friendships with other women I admired for many reasons, not least of which was their own capacity for self-acceptance) to persuade me that I had to face the fact that I was not such an odd creature, but simply a woman with qualities both good and bad, like everyone else. A fractured, divided person, driven by the goal of integration.

To become an integrated person—one able to recognize and accept all parts of herself, good or bad: Maybe this sounds like a peculiar goal, as its achievement comes without ceremony or fancy brass statues. But it's a worthwhile pursuit nevertheless, for many reasons, only one of which is this: While the dichotomy between good and bad remains a public-private division for women, while we resist the integration that makes these divisions obsolete, we will never be able to make ourselves wholly available in the manner that genuine intimacy with another person demands. And so we will remain caught in our own solitary and falsely ordered world, lamenting our lack of a satisfying relationships even as we carefully maintain the absence of self-knowledge and acceptance that are the very obstacles to romantic and personal fulfillment.

If anyone had told me during the early months of my relationship with my beau—a hectic period during which I attempted to juggle the logistical demands of a new relationship with a seemingly endless number of time-intensive multiple-process hair-coloring treatments—that all the anxiety and panic I was experiencing would be the easy part, I'm sure I would have shot that person. But, dead or alive, that person would have been right. Oh, sure, I developed an ulcer convincing myself that each of our dates would be the last one and torn ligaments developing an acrobatic technique that could deliver me discreetly from the bed to the bathroom, but, during love's incipient phase, I was just doing what I always did: having a grand old time with myself. Yes, something told me that this time was different, but I certainly wasn't about to listen. I just marched along ignoring the reality of the situation— the fact that this man was actually serious—and set about simultaneously objectifying my beau into my usual romantic antihero and steeling myself for the moment when the whole thing would blow up in my face. It had happened before, after all, each and every time. I had no reason to respect my own instincts or to be particularly trusting of my partner's.

At a certain point, and not without considerable regret, my little solipsistic adventure had to come to an end. After years of allowing pseudoboyfriends to mask the fact that my one great love was my own fertile imagination, this comfortable, self-contained fantasy world of mine was shattered by the actual presence of another person. And there were times when I just couldn't handle it.

This is no reflection on my beau. The brute luck I seem to have had in that department can only be attributed to karmic recompense—God must have an excellent seat in the theater of my romantic disasters. It is, however, a reflection on me, specifically on the investment I had in protecting my insular emotional life. The most formidable challenge I faced in my relationship was not getting past the fourth date or finally confessing that the distension of my abdomen had nothing to do with water weight gain. The biggest challenge was—and is—trying to bring down the barriers that I spent so many years constructing to safeguard my solitude. When confronted with a topic that's painful or difficult, even if I know its exploration is essential to the progress of the relationship, my first and powerful instinct is to withdraw, to disappear into myself. Only now, after years of practice, can I be persuaded that attentiveness, rather than escape, is the more productive response to a problem or conflict. Which is certainly not to suggest that I always choose productivity, only that I now recognize that the choice of either route—attention or avoidance—is all mine.

Here's the sentence you've all been waiting for: You have much more control over your romantic situation than you think. Your romantic fate is in your own hands to a staggering degree. And it has nothing to do with what you wear or your haircut or the clever conversational party tricks you've taught yourself. Your romantic fate will be determined by your relationship with yourself.

Once you make the decision to know yourself, once you devote yourself to serious self-exploration—affirming those parts you're proud of or pleased by, examining those parts that may displease or worry you—you start to lose the ability to deceive yourself. No longer will you be able to convince yourself that the only salient factor in your romantic encounters is whether a particular guy happens to like you. Instead, you'll begin to consider these encounters in terms of your own response: Does this person sustain your interest? Are you attracted to him? Is he even worth your time?

Once you begin to accept that romantic attraction is an actively reciprocal sport, it becomes almost impossible to lie to yourself, whether about your own potential interest in an individual or his in you. When the mutual sparks are there, you'll know it. When they're not, you'll leave tracks.

There's an almost insultingly simple rule about romantic engagement, so simple that we habitually overlook it as we pound love's pavement, and it is this: If it is meant to be, it will be. If it's not, it won't. As one who spent all of her pre–Loving Care days in a near psychotic effort to bend the wills of reluctant romantic partners, this rule exists in direct opposition to practically every romantic move I ever made. And yet it's true. If the object of your interest doesn't want to get involved, there's not a push-up demi-cup bra, elective surgical procedure, or dramatic alteration of your personality that's going to make him change his mind. And if said object wants in, so to speak, there's no moronic thing you can do—throw up in his car, smile after eating a poppy-seed bagel, have a hysterical pregnancy—to deter him from his desired course. You can neither force something that's not meant to be nor screw up something that is.

In other words, the only control you have is over yourself. Which means that however you construe happiness—be it piloting an airplane (although any sane person knows that metal is heavier than air), taking to the stage, camping out on the Serengeti, digging for artifacts in Nepal, or even finding a partner to commit to and make a life with—achieving this goal is entirely within your power. And the degree to which you're able to be honest with yourself will dictate the accuracy with which you choose and pursue the goals that give life (even a life in which gay men are better looking than straight men) real meaning. If you find that your singular goal seems to be the snaring of an elusive or phantom partner, chances are your relationship with yourself is in an estranged state. Do something about it. Ask yourself out. A little wining and dining, a bunch of flowers, some overpriced Belgian chocolate. By all means, fall in love. It'll be the start of a relationship with a guaranteed future.